SUBCONSCIOUS SPECTRUMS TO GOD-CONSCIOUSNESS

Christine 'little chrissy' Brinkley

BALBOA.PRESS
A DIVISION OF HAY HOUSE

Balboa Press books may be ordered through booksellers or by contacting:

Balboa Press
A Division of Hay House
1663 Liberty Drive
Bloomington, IN 47403
www.balboapress.com
844-682-1282

Because of the dynamic nature of the Internet, any web addresses or links contained in this book may have changed since publication and may no longer be valid. The views expressed in this work are solely those of the author and do not necessarily reflect the views of the publisher, and the publisher hereby disclaims any responsibility for them.

The author of this book does not dispense medical advice or prescribe the use of any technique as a form of treatment for physical, emotional, or medical problems without the advice of a physician, either directly or indirectly. The intent of the author is only to offer information of a general nature to help you in your quest for emotional and spiritual well-being. In the event you use any of the information in this book for yourself, which is your constitutional right, the author and the publisher assume no responsibility for your actions.

Any people depicted in stock imagery provided by Getty Images are models, and such images are being used for illustrative purposes only.
Certain stock imagery © Getty Images.

Scripture quotations marked KJV are from the Holy Bible, King James Version (Authorized Version). First published in 1611. Quoted from the KJV Classic Reference Bible, Copyright © 1983 by The Zondervan Corporation.

Print information available on the last page.

ISBN: 978-1-9822-5621-0 (sc)
ISBN: 978-1-9822-5622-7 (e)

Balboa Press rev. date: 10/09/2020

*Dedicated to Humanity seeking Truths, Peace, Joy and
Unconditional Love connection to Families, Nature and Source*

. . . and to Ronald . . .

Perhaps the only limits to the human mind are those we believe in"—**Willis Harman** (Aug 16, 1918-Jan 30, 1997)

Let's consider—**The Laws of the Universe** (Part One, first 12 chapters) as **Infinite-Energies** with **Infinite possibilities** that expose Humanity's outdated thinking within **The Laws of Karma** (Part Two, last 12 chapters) . . . But what if Humanity's thinking is/was over 170% OUT-OF-SYNC with those of *God's Potentiality and Intent* (Intent, as a powerful enforcer of ALL of the Laws)? Now, let's consider how far Willis Harman's previous statement about the human mind if it is also 170-180% out-of-sync with those Energies of *Nature's Potentiality, also expressed as Human Subconscious?*

> *"The knowing of one's Self can open many doors. More than a simple step—it is a Quantum Leap with the simple leading to chaotic complexity. But you have to sow if you wish to reap."*
> (one of The Laws of Karma)

This book is a personal journey of discovery into the Subconscious mind. Respect and love yourself, Beautiful Soul. If ever you feel overwhelmed, I recommend skipping immediately to the **Wisdom Appendix** and read any of it!

SLOW DOWN; THINGS WILL GO FASTER!

CONTENTS

PART ONE

TRUTHS: LAWS OF THE UNIVERSE

Until 2020, I humbly never understood my 9 years of journal-like writings, 2006-2015. For the reason—14 years ago I was same as my neighbor no matter how far apart we are/were geographically. For the reason—5 years ago, 2015, a massive stroke stripped me of 100% Academics and 100% memories, walking from the hospital into sunlight. I began again at birth emotionally and mentally. (*Now, I don't recall writing any of the 9 years of journaling: I have included them in this book because I Know they are mine.*) Besides the brain and body I had my Subconscious Super-Computer-Cosmic-to-Source-Energy flow. Source makes the heart feel warm and Freedom rings like rose petals on your cheeks as tears—glorious, breathtaking, sharing love. Yet to be productive I Knew I had to relearn everything; TWO beginnings in ONE lifetime is humbling. I prayed a lot.

If it is right for you to have, hear, See or experience something, it is the right thing to pray for it. Prayer is a realization of the God-power within you. Prayer is not asking of favors: Kingdom of Heaven is within each of us.

> Pythagoras (570 B.C.E. TO 500-490 B.C.E.)—
> *"Man Know thyself,*
> *then thou shall Know*
> *the Universe and God."*

1

<u>Sensitivities</u>—RECOMMEND THAT <u>ALL 3</u> AGREE, OBSERVER BEING

1. Continue reading if you wish to change your life FOREVER?
2. Continue reading WHEN you are willing to let go of your Beliefs?
3. Continue reading if you are NOW **ready to take** RESPONSIBILITY **for your Life.**

PART ONE INTRODUCTION

HUMANITY'S TRUTHS

With inner Duty to all of Humanity, writing this book was a daunting task after a 2015 stroke impaired my brain. (Think of a stroke inside the brain as a MAJOR-GREY-MATTER EARTHQUAKE WIPING THE LANDSCAPE AS IT GOES.) Nonetheless, the stroke gave me experiences since 2015 that not many have known. I did **walk** out the hospital doors into bright sunshine 4-days later. I was forever changed as a walking-talking miracle patient. So, who had I become WITHOUT MEMORIES OR ANY ACADEMICS? Definitely not human!)

My academics weren't all the accredited kind. Beyond an Associate's degree, my academics were a lifetime of learning, reading, studying anything put in front of me—Absorbing data. All gone except for an occasional-memory flashes that I, a Heyoka Empath cannot say for sure were actually mine. Any exhilaration normally felt by other authors after finishing a book went unnoticed. However, an ancient text *told me— "Look then at his words and all the writings which have been completed."* (Nag Hammadi Library in English, HarperCollins Publisher, James M. Robinson, 1990, *The Thunder: Perfect Mind*, p 303) I have tried to do that looking for Truths that sync with Subconscious' Truths connecting me to God-Consciousness. For with or without memories or Academics, besides the body/brain, the Subconscious Super-Computer-Cosmic-to-Source-Energy flow was all there was left for me to work with. But how was I going to learn how to Know what it is telling me?

The Subconscious mind is NOT self-sabotaging. That is the Ego. The Subconscious mind is NOT the body. That is an accumulation of our own emotional responses, including food cravings, addictions, fights, injuries and all negative emotions lumped and knotted up inside your body year after year after year.

The Subconscious Super-Computer-Cosmic-to-Source-Energy flow mind CANNOT claim superiority over the Emotions. That again is the Ego. The Emotions are the conductor of the Subconscious that is overseen by the "I" AM, a powerful ruler of electromagnetic radiation (EMR) **that is the Subconscious mind**.

This book is my tough love to you, Dear Observer Beings, unconditionally. If I was made completely stupid and had to learn over and over and over again, which I had to do—I still Know the numerous energies of the Subconscious will test you beyond measure until you 'GET IT', _THEIR INTENT_ THAT IS. You'll find ideas duplicated and most times rephrased throughout, because repetition is what it takes until Nature's point is made, Observer-Beings. Embrace your Childside (Childishness), which is your direct link to God-Universe (_sometimes called 'Source'_). The same connection will let Humanity converse via extra-sensory perception (ESP) and through our heart with our Celestial families, Nature and Source.

Take responsibility for your life, and stop your Egotism's control so you can find your Authentic self, Purpose and the Holy Grail of our physiological quest—healing ourselves naturally. I will shed light on many complexities of the Subconscious that affects everyone in the Here and Now of Life. There is NOTHING GOOD OR BAD only what you, Observer-Being, allow in your mind. **Come as little children in awe of the wonders of everything, questioning everything along the way.**

None of my books were ever intended to be _about_ me. I wish to provide a language for understanding Humanity's inner dialogue. It is time for Humanity to answer the harder questions of our existence—WITHOUT PREJUDICE OR JUDGEMENT (both Intents will limit Human intelligence).

'The Lord helps them who help themselves' is the Truth.
The Subconscious has all the power. Period!
Have Faith in yourselves. Always!
If Faith is without words **and EMOTIONS**, then **Faith is gone**.

Man is his own fate. All humans See is Mind, and Mind is the only cause and effects there are! Seek first the Kingdom of God-Universe within you. Knock and it shall open up to you. Use it to think constructively. If <u>Thought plus</u> *good or bad* <u>Emotions equals Creation</u>, then we create our own realities **inside and outside us**. Then Humanity complains or protests about their woes. When you awake by Being Aware, then the answers you seek will be there.

SLOW DOWN; THINGS WILL GO FASTER!

Start by blocking doubts and fears, simply say, "NO NO NO!" All thoughts flashing through your mind are a fast moving scroll. Everybody is getting the same scroll except in different vibrations, different octaves of the bigger picture. This is the major reason this Subconscious Spectrums book is not about me; it is about the piece you can include within this Summary of the Subconscious that should thought of as a humbling *Starter Kit*.

Externally, Humanity was given dominion over the things of the Earth. Appreciation for Earth has been lacking since Humanity embraced the selfishness of Egotism. Everything about Egotism is about "me me me," but that construct is ending before 2020 ends. Thought is the conductor, Observer-Beings. Be careful your thoughts you put Emotion to, because <u>Thought and Emotion makes matter</u> (Creation), because every Action you put out, an equal action comes back. (*If your Ego wishes to blame-shift to someone or something outside of yourself that is showing you it is your Ego who is driving your motivations.*)

Humanity's only job is to connect to Source (God-Consciousness) by Knowing ourselves. I embrace my Soul's wholeness. End of each day I bless the records of the day with love before sending them onward. It is a daily cleansing our Emotions require. <u>Always remember this fact</u>.

Imagine yourself as any dog tied *out back* day-after-season-after year, alone without contact and love. I've seen hundreds of television advertisements for donations to help free you from the collar shackle around your neck. Until you are rescued from your shackle, you will stay cold every winter, parched every summer. Lonely. Hungry. Flea-bitten. Miserable. Feelings that are flooded with being **un**-Loved. How much more pain must you endure of this life before death grants you peace? You might not literally be a dog, but I guarantee your <u>inner shackles</u> are far worse than the poor abused animals shackled by Humanity's own hands all around the globe.

Yin-Yang balance is needed in our thinking to maintain elasticity in our uncertain, unpredictable future, a future potentially fraught with chaos as our galaxy realigns its electromagnetic forces. In the same way, Yin-Yang balance is needed to avoid structured brain-wiring, to build brain elasticity for a smarter Humanity. Perhaps Nature's fury occurs long enough for us to appreciate Nature's beauty when it comes, or perhaps it is motivation to create new beauty? Humanity's job is to ask questions. Question Everything.

Namaste, humbly with Peace Joy Truth and Unconditional Love, 'little chrissy'

1

LAW OF DIVINE ONENESS (NAMASTE*)

Nature is asking Homosapiens to function with Nature's innocent playfulness and childishness (innocent Childside inside us) that can be felt in bodies of water and within all of Nature's kingdoms, large and small. Since the beginning of everything, Egotism has wired our brains with NEGATIVITY (making humans easier to control). This makes it very difficult to experience the blessed Garden-of-Eden that Earth is *Becoming*. The NEGATIVITY also has damaging effects on our mental and physical bodies, our physiological health. (Follow Dr. Bruce Lipton's YouTube videos.)

Since making peace with my Subconscious, *the "I" AM of my existence*;

- I have silence of mind 99% of the time,
- a God-Universe connection to Source,
- a strong tie to all of Humanity for <u>unknown reasons</u> and
- a tie to Earth that is hard to explain right now.
- My brain's NEGATIVITY took writing affirmations 6-8hrs/day for 2-3 weeks (in 2019) in order to rewire it for everything POSITIVE. Afterward, I felt lighter.
- Feeling lighter made it easier for me to experience the **Divine** of my Subconscious energies.
- Nature's actuality of the power of electromagnetic radiation (EMR) is not about what is seen with the eyes, which can be distorted from interference of INHERITED OR LEARNED BRAIN-WIRING.

The electromagnetic effects of brain wiring can be seen in nightmares and nightly dreams, which arise with distortions of sight. Electromagnetic effects in Nature can be seen when birds fly in unison.

*"Philosophers from Plato onward have argued over the years about the nature of reality. Classical science is based on the belief that there exists a real external world whose properties are definite and independent of the observer who perceives them . . . Both observer and observed are parts of a world that has an objective existence, and any distinction between them has no meaningful significance. In other words, if you see a herd of zebras fighting for a spot in the parking garage, it is because there really is a herd of zebras fighting for a spot in the parking garage. All other observers who look will measure the same properties, and the herd will have those properties whether anyone observes them or not. In philosophy that belief is called **realism**."* [Stephen Hawking, <u>The Grand Design</u>, pp 41-42]

*"Today the equations that describe electric and magnetic fields are called Maxwell's equations. Few people have heard of them, but they are probably the most commercially important equations we know. <u>Not only do they govern the working of everything from household appliances to computers, but they also describe waves other than light, such as microwaves, radio waves, infrared light, and X-rays.</u> All of these differ from visible light in only one respect—their **wavelength**. Radio waves have wavelengths of a meter or more, while visible light has a wavelength of a few ten-millionths of a meter, and X-rays a wavelength shorter than a hundred-millionth of a meter. Our sun radiates at all wavelengths, but its radiation is most intense in the wavelengths that are visible to us. It's probably no accident that the wavelengths we are able to see with the naked eye are those in which the sun radiates most strongly: It's likely that our eyes evolved*

> *with the ability to* **detect electromagnetic radiation** *in that range precisely because that is the range of radiation most available to them."* (Stephen Hawking, <u>The Grand Design</u>, pp 91-92)

Eyesight can be limiting. Our Subconscious mind, like our sun, can harness the full range of EMR, demonstrated by infinite range of personalities, mental and physical disorders and all emotional experiences. Opponents of today's Sciences sometimes ridicule while proclaiming any breakthroughs are utterly impossible. "I", contrary to these opponents, will show breakthroughs are everywhere. The utterly impossible is the consensus required to see such breakthroughs as being nowhere. Therefore, if the lack of consensus among today's Sciences and Religions is ignored, then the scattered breakthroughs can be brought together to paint an utterly beautiful masterpiece of prose, painting the breakthrough into the Mind of humankind. I have a piece of a big puzzle of the Natural World. My coauthor and friend, Ronald Grafton, also has a piece of the puzzle. I can, therefore, surmise that everyone on this beautiful Earth also has a piece of the big puzzle of our existence. Hence, the reason I wrote that this book was never intended to be about me.

> *Jesus said, "When you disrobe without being ashamed and take up your garments and place them under your feet like little children and tread on them, then you will see the son of the living one, and you will not be afraid."* (The Nag Hammadi Library, James M. Robinson, HarperCollins, 1978, p 130)

To function *with Her splendor,* Nature is asking Humanity to know themselves from the inside, get rid of external motivations, get rid of negativity so as to attract positive things, such as joy, truth, peace and unconditional love (like energies attract like energies). Allow yourselves to go into a dream-like state (referenced as the 4th Dimension on YouTube) where every dream is possible with such a splendorous love for ourselves that we can fly.

* *

Seeing, *not with the eyes*, Seeing with our senses the words of our ancient ancestors can support our understanding of Nature's INTENT. Any conversations about the Subconscious mind should come from Humanity's heart. (Humanity's heart is smarter than our brains will ever be and 5,000 times more powerful in broadcasting energy.) In order to achieve a bigger picture of the workings of our Subconscious, every IDEA had to meet the standard—

- ✓ Facilitate The Sciences + Quantum Physics + Biology + Religions MERGING TOGETHER to be valid. *IF not—a warning flag is sent up, because all four exist in the same universe and should merge cohesively.* Any scientific experiment-results should stand up to rigors inherent in the basic laws of logic. Scientific considerations of test results should also shred out-dated ignorant superstitions, or poorly grounded constructs. For any discerning process, definitions and foundation-values are critical—

1. Think of **Science** in terms of Observations that meet sound logic and testing standards.
2. The playfulness of the **Nature** in **Quantum Physics** and **Intent of the Energies** contained in hydrogen atoms are observed in physics labs. I have sensed the same playfulness in the Gulf of Mexico ocean water. The water likewise showed me a green lattice overlaying the water that I felt from my heart that it was *Her* heart. Nature is about love for all of Life.
3. **Biology is a manifestation of Nature's Intent of energies inside our bodies** (*refer to Laws of Universe in chapter titles of Part One*) and the functioning relationship with those energies (*refer to your own physical health and the Laws of the Karma (chapter titles in Part Two*), and Evolution is their methodology—expressing **Intent** through Humanity's INDIVIDUAL actions, deeds, Emotions of Subconscious, heart and thoughts.
4. Religion is an **expression of the personal relationship** between Humanity and those energies physically expressing **_their_** Intent in Humanity's brain, mind and body.

These understandings made it easier for me to interpret the words of ancient philosopher's and scribes. They hold the keys to answering, "*Why is there Life?*" They are vital to understand and sense evolution as it affects each individual **Here and Now**—Not *some other place and time.*

We are our ancestors' academics, beliefs and brain-wiring. Ancient Gnostics were tuned-in to Nature's music, swirling thickly around humans every moment of every day. It is the Source of Human gut feelings. It can explain much about our existence, if we listen. Our body's physiology is fully equipped to hear all of it. The Subconscious can answer our physiological quest for the Holy Grail—something that resides inside us all. The only issue—Egotism is the wicked-villain, Satan, that attached Observer Beings to the 2nd highest frequency of EMR since *in the beginning.*

The atom was unstable *in the beginning*, nearly breaking apart, until God-Universe, *blew her 'breath'* on the atom. (From ancient text—*On the Origin of the World*, The Nag Hammadi Library) Read Ecclesiastes: "*Vanity of Vanities, said the Preacher, vanity of vanities; ALL it vanity.*" (1:2) 'True Man' will not come about until we become tuned-in with our Creativity Emotion—the Child in us, the lowest-frequency range of electromagnetic radiation (EMR). What is the reason? Simply put, our Ego's higher-frequency range has hijacked traits from the other six frequency ranges that have directly affected our physical health. **The higher a system functions the less stable it is.** (Ask any engineer or your automobile mechanic.)

Individually we are all humans with our own unique Emotional *Experiences* as part of Humanity the whole, also known as—Homosapiens. Since *the-beginning* Homosapiens functioned with Egotism and Vanity selfishly holding the reins of our motivations that we hid from everyone. Biological scientific testing has proven shocking negative results. (Follow Dr. Joe Dispenza's videos on YouTube.)

Ecclesiastes defines Egotism *Effects* in everything, everywhere, everyone, everytime; Egotism is described with precision in texts about *"Goodness, Ignorance and Passion"* in the Bhagavad-Gita (as DISGUISES/DECOYS ABOUT EGOTISM)

Egotism's cycle is ending. **Earth** is a *Planetary* **Being** *who is* traveling at tens-of-thousands of kilometers per hour through space while it's stretching out after a 26,000-year cycle ending December 2020). EarthBeing's core has evolved into a 5th-Dimension-*higher* vibration that Humanity can feel as Joy, Truth, Peace and Unconditional Love. Earth-Being **is** shaking off anything not at least of the fourth dimension-higher vibration felt as the ***dream-state.*** Below is a list of Egotism's control over the other Emotions of the Subconscious. It is this emotional HIJACKING that is preventing Humans from healing themselves.

- Our Ego and Vanity took over the Righteous side of our Righteous Emotion and turned it into arrogance and self-righteousness.
- Our Ego and Vanity have hijacked the presumption side of our Presumption emotion to make our Ego and Vanity <u>feel good</u> by making us believers of cruelty-to-others falsehoods. Presumption has been the #1 sin of humans.
- Our Ego and Vanity turned our Sadness into self-pity, spreading our Creativity thinner and thinner with every passing year. This explains why breakthroughs are difficult to discover, making science writer John Horgan's books successful. Humankind has lost the ability to look *outside the box* beyond our <u>confirmation bias</u> (beliefs or constructs) and <u>cognitive dissonance</u> (academics and/or brain-wirings).
- Our Ego and Vanity converted our Obsession emotion into obsessive compulsive disorders, along with various obscene obsessions, and made her Sloth side a sin, or uses Sloth as an excuse to be lazy. What is so wrong with taking a little relaxing downtime with Nature?
- Our Ego and Vanity controlled our humble little Beings by using the Fear side of our Happiness emotion against us. How can anyone learn to know Happiness through such control?
- Our Ego and Vanity uses the Dread side of our Hope emotion also as an excuse to be lazy. Dread, therefore, doesn't have a chance to shine with her strength—acting as an advisor for the most efficient means to accomplish any task, if only we had a brain with Patience.

In early 2008, with the help of my friend Ronald Grafton, a Mid-west tree farmer, I was connected to my Subconscious through a process requiring Knowledge, preparation and logic, while **simultaneously squelching every tendency toward making fast reactions to the goings-on in my Mind**. Another friend of mine, Steve Kaplan, had asked, "How do you know you broke through to your Subconscious mind?" I know because I can describe the VEIL that acts as an opaque and obscure rear-projection television, projecting distorted images in front of it that we see as realities. I know because I can describe my experiences as the VEIL gradually became translucent. I know because the VEIL grew more and more transparent until it vanished altogether, showing me what was behind it; mostly blackness, save for black-on-black snapshots of seven Emotions, or snapshots of other energies in action, whatever the chaotic "I" AM of the Subconsciou would allow. The Mayan's called them [the energies], "Lords of the Underworld." The Egyptians called them "Ka." The Mayans also referenced Black-earth and Black-on-high, which is about quantum functions of the Subconscious Super-Computer-Cosmic-Energy-to-Source, whereby everything can eventually turn black when the lights go off. Blackness absorbs 100% of light.

> *"It is said that in developing his theory of relativity, Alberts Einstein imagined himself riding on a beam of light. Is this just a quaint anecdote about the creative process or is the mind truly capable of such a feat? There is scientific evidence from researchers at renowned universities that the mind can do even more than this. For example, studies at Stanford have shown that through our thoughts we can affect a distant person's blood pressure or heart rate. And scientists at Princeton have documented the mental communication of information from one person to another over distances of thousands of miles."* (The Emerging Mind, Karen Nesbitt Shanor, 1999, p ix) (cont'd from footnote 2) *In February 1994, at a Smithsonian seminar . . . The proof that such information could be communicated mentally from one person to another was interesting enough, but what really astounded the Smithsonian audience was that in a large number of cases, receivers got the information up to three days before it was sent.*

I love this sharing research of results that were extraordinary. Human vessel-bodies are pretty extraordinary. Life does Become 99% peaceful once we all shift our focus from reacting to every nonsensical noisy thought inside the head to real Feelings coming from the solar-plexus gut and the heart, *then throughout the body and head entire*. Makes me say, "Wow!" Life also gets easy. You are chilling-out reading this with gamma-amino butyric acid (GABA) clearing your brain of noise by <u>blocking all other receptors</u>. Quiet, huh? Yeah, it is a beautiful thing. Gentlemen and poker players, here is one snippet of Truth for you Beings—*Betting-on-the Come* is losing Faith in yourself.

As Earth speeds through space stretching out her newfound freedom, all Subconscious energies are pouring into Humanity's reality whether you can see them or not. Extreme caution and **Patience** must be used in order to maintain sanity. This is best explained by Carlos Castaneda (December 25, 1925?–April 27, 1998). Castaneda wrote books, narrated in first person, describing his training in traditional Mesoamerican shamanism, and the events before and after meeting a Yaqui shaman don Juan Matus in 1960. The most significant fact in a person's life, according to Castaneda, is in elevating one's dormant Awareness. The same heightened Awareness also becomes the primary goal of a warrior, referred to many times by don Juan. On August 20, 1961, don Juan told Castaneda, *"A man goes to Knowledge as he goes to war, wide-awake, with fear, with respect, and with complete assurance. Going to Knowledge or going to war in any other manner is a mistake, and whoever makes it will live to regret his steps."* (The Teachings of Don Juan, 43)

Castaneda argues that everything we perceive, feel and how we act is determined by the position of an *assemblage point* whereby conscious movement of it permits perception of the world in different ways, a non-ordinary reality. Ultimately, claims Castaneda, most adults can only move or shift their assemblage point in dreams or by way of drug use, love, hunger (fasting), fever, exhaustion, or through inner silence. Today's energy is different—more cooperative with Egotism on its way out!

Greek philosopher Plotinus (205-270 AD) described the Soul of Man, in his Enneads, in the exact same way as the assemblage point referred to by don Juan. The importance of don Juan's description is that he equated it with our ability to **Observe—Awareness**. <u>YouTube</u> monk, Dandapani, explains Awareness as light movement around the mind/brain/body, exploring different parts to **Observe** what is there. donJuan pointed out the assemblage point could be both moved and shifted, such as when a person observes their own body during a near-death experience.

One day when I was strolling with a friend through the water's edge at Panama City Beach, the waves suddenly almost knocked us both down. I stood centered on my feet saying, "Down, down, calm, calm," with the palm of my hand facing the water. I felt playful at the time, June 2019. Here came the waves and I am still talking to it. The water actually quickly dropped brushing softly against our ankles. Made me giggle. So I did it again and again. The results were the same. The ocean and its inhabitants want to play, but Humanity isn't brain-wired for that yet! My assemblage point shifted again to See a green overlay of the Gulf of Mexico's heart lying on top of the water . . .

The shifting of the assemblage point can explain how a person observes certain phenomena in their brain, most likely what children are doing when they report successfully fighting cancer cells in their mind. People monitoring gut feelings shift their Awareness from the external to the internal, focusing on themselves. Poker players do it all the time. Try it by focusing your attention on how cold or warm you feel. As soon as you do this, you are focusing your Awareness inside you, Observer Beings.

To Know ourselves defined by ancient prophecies includes following advice of Jesus in the text of the Nag Hammadi Library, 'to become as little children' until we can feel the Source of all there is in God-Universe with such a infinite unconditional love for self that you feel you can fly!

> *"And said, Verily I say unto you, Except ye be converted, and become as little children ye shall not enter into the kingdom of heaven."* —Mathew: 18-3

Emphasize the validity of don Juan's warning for going to Knowledge and to war—wide awake, with fear and respect. Be very wise and CAUTIOUS if your Egotism attempts ANY boasting. If you want to know exactly how chaotic and POWERFUL the "I" is, then read the poem, "**The Thunder Perfect Mind**" of the Nag Hammadi Library, which will be used throughout this book and future books I write.

"**For many**
 are the pleasant forms which
 exist in numerous sins (OF EGOTISM),
 and incontinencies (OF EGOTISM),
 and disgraceful passions (OF EGOTISM),
 and fleeting pleasures (OF EGOTISM),
 which men (AND WOMEN)**, embrace**
 until they (BEINGS)**, become sober** (MAKE PEACE WITH
BALANCED EMOTIONS) **and**
 go up ('UP' IS A DECOY—LOW ENERGY STATES ARE
PREFERRED) **to their resting place.**
 And they will find
 me (THE "I" AM OF THE SUBCONSCIOUS—IS THE
SUBCONSCIOUS) **there, and they will**
 live, and they will not die again." —The Nag
Hammadi Library in English, p303. **Namaste . . .**

About personal **FREEDOM:** We can give ourselves permission to Feel our Emotions. Give ourselves permission to just BE in the NOW, where you are sitting/standing, feel the air around you. Close your eyes and feel your Emotions (Independent Events) and feel your body (your physical vessel for this lifetime). Just have FAITH in YOU, Beautiful Souls; we will get through this together.

A movie *The Legend of Bagger Vance* was played by actor Will Smith. Will is explaining to a golfer about how to feel aligned with the **'Field'** to make an authentic golf shot. I'm providing Will's lines applicable to functioning with Subconscious contained in the atom by replacing specific values.

> *"Look at life thus far as a practice searching for something. Then find yourself right into the middle of it, feeling the focus of a lot of shots to choose from, but there's only one shot that's in perfect harmony with the Field. One that's the Authentic Shot, and that Shot is going to choose you. There's a perfect Shot out there trying to find each and every one of us. All we got to do is get ourselves out of its way. Let it choose us.*

> *Can't see it as some dragon you have to slay, Egotists. You got*
> *to look with soft eyes, Child-side of Humans. See the place*
> *where the tides and seasons and turning of the Earth all come*
> *together where everything that IS becomes One. You got to*
> *seek that place with your Soul. Don't think about it. Feel it.*
> *Seek it with your heart. Your heart is wiser than your head is*
> *ever going to be.* I can't take you there. Just hope I can help*
> *you find a way. That Field and all you are; seek it with your*
> *heart. Don't think about it. Feel it. You're looking at it: Your*
> *Authentic Self, that Field and all that you are."* (*Science has
> measured our heart as being 5,000 times stronger energy
> than the mind.)

The Subconscious is a reality of constantly changing unknowns and unpredictable possibilities. Everything perceived sensation must be considered as just a small piece of a much larger picture—our individualistic entity. Whatever we experience at any given point in time is real, and whatever our body and Subconscious senses and goes through is real. However, that does not mean we immediately realize its Actuality or purpose. **Temporary-home everything, Observer Being.**

Nature used numerical mathematics to develop today's technologies, such as putting man on the moon, computers, power stations, the Web, atom colliders, etcetera. These same technologies empower scholars to examine Nature as far as our current technologies can provide knowledge of 'Her'. Yet we have reached a point of diminishing returns. Mankind must begin looking beyond what we can see with our eyes, eyes of a very limited range of electromagnetic radiation (EMR).

So, if we have not experienced something, then can we properly predicate the outcome? Secret society members can describe the 'quantum weirdness zoo' of our Subconscious—if they hadn't sworn an oath of secrecy. They could also explain how much time and trouble it takes during their initiations to break in to their Subconscious. But the "I" of our mind decides the final outcome. She decides who stays and who goes. She decides what information gets passed through the Cosmic Internet of the Cosmos (IOTC, is what I call it), as in the Princeton experiment, *or not.* "I" is always present in everything humankind or the animal kingdom does.

She decides our fate based on the personal responsibility shown through our actions. She decides whether to make our live miserable or not, usually based on whether our Ego/Vanity gets in Her way to fulfill Nature's Intent for us. Everything in the physical world is made of Atoms. Everything in the physical world is made of Atoms. Atoms are made of energy: Energy is made out of Consciousness . . .

—from *The Thunder: Perfect Mind*, Nag Hammadi Library:

For many are the pleasant forms [endorphin highs-fast spinning gravitons-latched onto by Beings]

which exist in
    numerous sins (from Egotism),
    and incontinencies (from Egotism),
    and disgraceful passions (from Egotism),
    and fleeting pleasures (from Egotism),
which (men) embrace until they [Beings] *become sober* [balanced]
    and go up [up is a decoy—should be down!] *to their resting place.*

> *And they will find me there* [**the "I"**—Perfect Mind/ Heaven on Earth]*, and they will live, and they will not die again* [the soul breaks apart] *up* [up is a decoy-should be down—Low Energy State like chillin' out!]

> *to their resting place* [low energy state to rebalance neurotransmitters; sensed as depression to Beings]

Hope and Survival

Nature will NOT choose everyone, survival of the fittest (*I am guessing*). Nonetheless, all Beings can choose to change with Nature or choose to stay in their pathetic state of Ego-existing. I say, "Take your time." Nature agrees with this message: "Slow down, things will go faster." I know this works *in Nature's analog world I function in,* but I don't know why? It must be a *law of physics thing*. Nonetheless, one of the most important messages from the Bhagavad Gita will help immensely, *"When your intelligence has passed out of the dense forest of delusion (Ego-control), you shall become indifferent to all that has been heard and all that is to be heard."* Bg 2.52

NOTES: Evolution and Creationism are the same thing. The only thing exterior to our Subconscious mind and our physical vessel-body is skin color—**Skin color is irrelevant**! We are all One, infinite Beings, extensions of Source, God-Universe.

The hardest part for most people is tuning out brain wiring (confirmation bias-*sticking to whatever beliefs you always cling to and noisy academic thoughts*—cognitive dissonance). **Everything in the physical world is made of Atoms. Atoms are made of energy: Energy is made out of Consciousness . . .**

> *"It is said that in developing his theory of relativity, Alberts Einstein imagined himself riding on a beam of light. Is this just a quaint anecdote about the creative process or is the mind truly capable of such a feat? There is scientific evidence from researchers at renowned universities that the mind can do even more than this. For example, studies at Stanford have shown that through our thoughts we can affect a distant person's blood pressure or heart rate. And scientists at Princeton have documented the mental communication of information from one person to another over distances of thousands of miles."* (The Emerging Mind, Karen Nesbitt Shanor, 1999, p ix)

A linkup to The Field, which is above our heads about at arm-length, is similar, but different from Webbot data. It is cleaner and clearer, easier to comprehend in the middle of the night when there are less technological interferences.

More breakthroughs can be discovered when humans STOP worrying about *who gets the credit, PERIOD*. Screaming for credit arises from Humanity's Egotism of our cognitive dissonance (academics) and/or confirmation bias (beliefs). Academics and <u>beliefs with emotional ties</u> clog the body with dis-ease.

"The nobler Soul will have the greater power; the poorer Soul, the lesser. A soul which defers to the bodily temperament cannot escape desire and rage (Egotism) *and is abject in poverty, overbearing in wealth, arbitrary in power* (all Egotism). *The soul of nobler nature holds well against its surroundings* (Natural settings); *it is more apt to change them than to be changed, so that often it improves the environment and, where it must make concession, at least keeps its innocence* (Childishness). *"* [Ennead 3.1.8] Enneads are the philosophical writings of Plotinus (205-270 AD) a pupil of Plato's University.

The Universal greeting—Namaste' means

"My Soul honors your Soul. I honor the place in you where the Universe Entire resides. I honor the light, love, truth, beauty and place within you, because it is also within me. In sharing these things we are united, we are the same, we are ONE." *Namaste . . .*

2

LAW OF VIBRATION

Aligning with the Childishness of our Subconscious also aligns us to Source, directly to God-Universe. This alignment rids Humanity of Egotism. Evolution asks us to return to our infancy when our innateness was pure, when our innocence felt amazement, awe about everything in life that made us question everything with Joy, Truth, Peace and Unconditional Love. This is the 5th dimension-higher vibration we need to survive the huge shift we are Being asked to make. The 4th dimension-higher vibration is a helpful **dream-state** where the Divine Subconscious can align with you. Learn to Be Responsible for yourself with Duty and Need; let yourself align with Childishness and Resolve to align with Truths and Unconditional Love for everything.

Volumes of cosmic radiation pounding Earth as she speeds through space is freeing Humanity's memories of lower-3rd-dimension vibration from our karmic-debt lives. This helps us ease into becoming **baby Citizens of the Universe**. Not an easy task. Formidable! That's alright. We can do this together. Let's begin with nothingness, except what's in your **dream-state** imagination. What are you driving, or flying? Where are you going? What are you doing that you always loved to do? Who are you with? What are you wearing? Smelling? Feeling? Sensing? There is only now!

As we start feeling like Citizens of the Universe, everyday living becomes easier, calm and stress-free as people begin functioning with heartfelt purpose. Earth is happily sharing her heart with the **New**

Humanity. The contents page of this book should make it easier to see our transition from a list of how energy moves and grows. The 12 Laws of the Universe work together in harmonious rhythms-*turning-into cycles* within our Subconscious as the chariot drivers to God-Universe and life.

Briefly explaining them, but not in any particular order. Everything is energy that can be changed, moved or transformed, never destroyed. **Nothing happens outside of these Laws.** Imagine a GIANT LATTICE connecting us from our hearts to the whole Universe and all energy weaves in and throughout the lattice, all connected. That is—

1) **The Law of Divine ONENESS (Namaste)** connecting us to all of life throughout everywhere. Humans might not YET be able to FEEL the multitudes of energies swirling thickly around them 24/7. All it takes to tune-in is FOCUSED INTENT to KNOW THYSELF AND THE SUBCONSCIOUS WILL LISTEN!

2) **The Law of Vibration** tells us that negativity attracts negativity and positive energy attracts positive energy—thoughts, feelings, beliefs and actions. (Be careful what you think.)

3) **The Law of Action**—We must be doing something even if we are chilling out. Sloth is not a sin, but is actually one of our Dearest Emotions.

4) **The Law of Correspondence** SHOWS us what is inside of us because the SAME THING IS OUTSIDE OF US—OUR AURA.

5) **The Law of Cause and Effect** of all thoughts, feelings, beliefs and actions WILL COME BACK TO US, GOOD OR BAD IN THE SAME WAY POSITIVE AND NEGATIVE ENERGIES ATTRACT OR REPEAL ENERGIES.

6) **The Law of Compensation** brings us love and rewards for our inspirational deeds/actions AS PER OUR VIBRATIONS of Peace, Truth, Joy and Unconditional Love we emit from our hearts.

7) **The Law of Attraction** requires us to **have faith in ourselves** while we evolve into our Authentic Self, if not already there.

8) **The Law of Perpetual Transmutation of Energy** gives consciousness the capacity to transform energies, such as thinking, into anything our Beings desire within the frequency of LOVE.

9) **The Law of Polarity** lets us choose to change from one lower mental vibration to another vibration even if opposites. Our Beings CHOOSE,

except for depression when our system throws us into depression for our neurotransmitters to rebalance, a perfect time to chill-out!

10) **The Law of Relativity** tells us we WILL face challenges, lessons, for us to learn who we are by our reactions to changes in our lives. People move in and out of our lives are/were here to serve as instigators for lessons our Souls are meant to learn during the current life.

11) **The Law of Rhythm** says energies have their own rhythms, rhythms become cycles; energies perpetually move in circular cycles. Think of an invisible-gigantic lattice connected from your heart center where energy is moving in and throughout the Universe.

12) **The Law of Gender** says everything has masculine and feminine potentials that our Being can choose to balance between Yin (masculine) and Yang (feminine) energy.

* * * * * * * * * * * * * * * * * * * *

Thought PLUS+ Emotion EQUALS= Creation

Thought + Emotion = Creation given that everything visible and invisible throughout the Universe is energy. Energy constantly exchanges data/information and is cyclical.

> Truth for instance is energy.
> Truth is usually hard to See, except instinctively.
> And yet Truth can be felt within our sensitive bodies and especially our hearts.

Since *In The Beginning*—Egotism was the system's ground that made up our souls. We were the grounding connection. We are programmed to hide Egotism's agendas in everything from war to peace. Egotism's Sneakiness bombed Pearl Harbor, kicking off America's war declaration. Egotism's revenge created the atomic blasts on Japan. Egotism's control created the Holocaust of loving people who knew God-Universe resides within them. They did not understand external expressions of God while still under Egotism's motivational control. Egotism is greed.

Memories & Academics equals who, what, where, when, how and why behind everything you do. Humans are programmed to hide Ego's agenda, forgetting how to speak bluntly like little children say what they mean from their hearts. Egotism's hidden agendas label all of Humanity as UNTRUSTWORTHY TO OUR CELESTIAL FAMILIES.

* * * * * * * * * * * * * * * * * * * *

Ancient Vedic expression—

> *"As in the microcosm (tiny), so is the macrocosm (vast).*
> *As in the atom, so is the universe.*
> *As in the human body, so is the cosmic body.*
> *As in the human mind, so is the cosmic mind."*

In sync with this ancient saying:

- Planet Earth has a spinning iron core.
- The hydrogen atom can also be imagined to have a spinning core, I once sensed as the spinning Tasmania-devil cartoon character.
- I sense as our Beings will *gravitate-to-anything*.
- Beings are gullible due to NEGATIVITY inherited/pre-wired in our brains.
- Beings have been addicted to high-energy endorphin highs and Hail-Mary's who have been **reactionary** Observers.

Time is now for Humanity to turn around and start paddling downstream. Start doing the easy—just **Observing**. Observing is when you 'sense' hunger in your gut, for instance. There are gazillions of sensors within us, if we just tune-in.

- Beings can CHOOSE to react or not!
- Beings can CHOOSE to keep our Awareness within ourselves.
- Beings have not yet realized self-empowerment when we can CHOOSE to maintain our inward focus even when someone's energy comes close to us.
- Beings can CHOOSE to ignore negativity when the brain spits it at us.

- Beings can CHOOSE to WILL AWAY any thoughts, feelings, interruptions, other people, everything that is NOT ALIGNING WITH US—EXCEPT WITH EARTH ENERGY!

The Earth has an atmosphere, part of which we breathe. The atom's atmosphere is the electron-field wavefunction, think of all as **information broadcasters**, sensed as our Awareness. (We feel other people's Awareness as their aura; also Nature's methodology for data transfer.) The Earth has Consciousness and we have consciousness, too. Then the hydrogen atoms we are made of must also have consciousness. **Everything in the physical world is made of Atoms. Atoms are made of energy: energy is made out of Consciousness.** Consciousness spreads throughout our systems into every cell. Our Subconscious, the "I" AM of our existence, is the Divine of Life. But then again we have been at war with *Her Nature* since Egotism has controlled Life . . .

As human citizens of Earth, you and I are assumed to be part of an apparently emotional Humanity. Or are we emotional Earthlings to Celestial Beings? Or perhaps we can be both? Perhaps a third possibility arises—the *otherworldly*, not-of-our control Emotions. Either way we are all Beings on planet Earth separated by our Emotional <u>Experiences</u> that seem to *be Otherworldly*, not of our control. Emotions are wavelengths. **Wavelengths defined by Webster's dictionary are nouns:**

1. **a series of colors arranged by wavelengths;** (*our Emotions are also arranged by wavelengths such as seen in seven colors of rainbows*)
2. **a line of thought that reveals a common understanding.**

Our common understanding is that we are all Beings here to serve ourselves as humble observers. Observers are like the sheep dog sitting calmly on the hill overseeing his sheep without reactions to every word and action that comes to mind. Take in every NOW moment, like the smells in the air, the sounds of wind through the grasses and trees. The sheep are calm, too. These are all external Observations. <u>So the Observer's job is only half done!</u>

The other half of the job is more difficult because of Emotional Experiences that are otherworldly and out-of-control. NOW is all that matters. Now Observer Beings, our Emotions are the otherworldly part of you that ARE LOUD, but so is your Observer *Reactionary* Being. Are you forgetting you can CHOOSE to NOT react to words and actions in the mind? Nonetheless, nothing can make us change our minds about something faster than external events blamed on creating Fear, Lies, Hate and Death. All four are usually targets of those people controlling populations and events, making most people puppets to other Humans.

In today's times we can have all four present on our insides if we **choose** to. I once did, but not since the stroke. Since then—I no longer detect any within me except for the occasional hint of Hate that doth protect my Self. Nonetheless, it sure is LOUD in THE FIELD, located above our heads. I do hear the Subconscious minds crying out. Vibrations of energy can be powerful with the force of billions of Beautiful Souls on the planet.

FEAR inside our minds and bodies shut off our immune system. Yes— OFF completely. (See YouTube videos of Dr. Joe Dispenza and Dr. Bruce Lipton) Fear puts our bodies in a state of flight and/or fight, and since the body cannot heal us at the same time, shuts down our immune system just like stress or fretting over depression. Beings CHOOSE whether to feel the stressor or not. But when it comes to flight or fight, the adrenaline rush is taken under the control of our Subconscious that shuts OFF consciousness and takes over the self-preservation. Given that our hearts are 5,000 times more powerful than our minds, the Childishness of our Subconscious is the direct link to our hearts and God-Universe (Source).

HATE is an Emotion of our childishness that can be felt by young and old alike to protect our quantum self from harm. THIS Childishness is the inner faith that we can do anything! Childishness is best described by a song of music group, (YouTube) FEARLESS SOUL, called "Thoughts Become Things" and because its words ring TRUTH, and is available on YouTube. Even the title is important for your thoughts do become things coming back at you according to the Laws of the Universe.

Be careful what you think—good or bad—it will come back to you. The song reminds you of when you were young before you got caught up in the Race-Race of Life. Take time to yourself to listen to the words of that song. It should do the Observer Being good!

Observer Beings—literally everything in the Universe is wavelengths of varied energy. Everything about Humanity is varied energy—good or bad. As a whole I prefer to think of Humanity as good but possibilities are not so cut and dry as that, because Egotism still exists.

> *"For I say, through the Grace given unto me, to every man that is among you, to think of himself more highly than he ought to think; but to think soberly**, according as God hath dealt to every man the measure of faith*."* (Romans 12:1-3)
>
> *FAITH IN SELF; **SOBERLY to our Subconscious Emotions is meant as—**Balance.**

Every one of our Emotions has experienced the same as you, Observer Beings. Hence, your Emotions give you plenty of head noise that Science predicts some 70,000-80,000 thoughts per day.

- Balanced Emotions takes focus, Beautiful Souls.
- Balanced Emotions bring Peace, Joy, Truth and Unconditional Love with direct link to Source.
- To get through the inner focus needed to find Balance, you might cry and not yet know why?
- OBSERVE—You may have words spill from your lips not knowing where they come from?
- OBSERVE—You might have many experiences you cannot explain **while** you are experiencing them?
- Keep ASKING questions, and keep asking until the answers start making your heart flutter?
- Observer Beings because with FAITH in yourself, you can find the answers you are seeking. Also, keep the twelve Laws of the Universe in mind and heart to receive consistent ABUNDANCE that is available to each of Humanity.

Removing hate from the big picture is difficult because it's a piece of our innateness. Removing hate leaves us with the Fear, Lies and Death.

DEATH is everywhere around us from microscopic to life size. Death tells us to evolve WITHOUT FEAR. WITHOUT FEAR our immune systems turn ON. When our immune systems are ON, we can begin to see the Lies that are everywhere, has been the same illusions Humanity has told itself since forever, along with addictions to drama, Drama, and DRAMA.

"I am not addicted to Drama," you say! If not, then why are you stressing during a powerful era of Humans **sharing Knowledge and Creativity**? Never are you stressing about Other People and their External problems of FEAR, LIES, HATE, sickness and DEATH? It is in the NEWS, RIGHT?

If you are one of the many who are stressed, perhaps you may consider rereading this chapter, Beautiful Soul, before proceeding, because your Ego/Vanity has you convinced you are perfectly happy controlling everyone/thing around you to please your way? What happens when you turn around to find someone to control, and there is **NO ONE** to be found—in the NEAR future?

—Hello, HUMILITY—

Wavelengths:

1. a series of colors arranged by wavelengths;
2. a line of thought that reveals a common understanding.

The other half of our job is more difficult because of Emotional Experiences, arising from our Emotions that are described as OTHERWORLDLY and out-of-control. NOW is all that matters! Now Observer Beings, our Emotions are the OTHERWORLDLY part of you that ARE VERY LOUD, but so is your Observer *Reactionary* Being.

Nonetheless, nothing can make us change our minds about something faster than external events blamed on creating Fear, Lies, Hate and Death. All four are usually targets of those people controlling populations and events, making most people puppets to other Humans.

In today's times we can have all four present on our insides if we **choose** to. I once did, but not since the stroke. Since then—I no longer detect any within me except for the occasional hint of Hate that doth protect my Self. Nonetheless, it sure is LOUD in THE FIELD, located above our heads. I do hear the Subconscious minds crying out. Vibrations of energy can be powerful with the force of billions of Beautiful Souls on the planet.

From (<u>The Secret of the World as laid down by the Secret Societies</u>, Mark Booth, 2008, The Overlook Press, p 400—

> *"When it comes to contemplating such far-flung events as the beginning of the Universe, it is inevitable that huge amounts of speculation are mapped on to the smallest conceivable specks of evidence. Leading physicists', cosmologists' and philosophers' speculations on infinite interlocking dimensions, parallel universes and 'soap-bubble universes' involve just as much imagination as Aquinas's speculations about angels on a pinhead. The point is that when it comes to the biggest questions, people are again not necessarily choosing according to the balance of the probabilities, which may be almost too small to measure. The world is like the 'perspected' picture that can equally well be seen as a witch or a pretty girl. People often choose one world-view in preference to another because somewhere in the depths of their Being that is what they WANT to believe. If we can become aware of this predisposition, we can make a decision which is—to that extent—free, because it is a decision based on knowledge. The part of us, somewhere in our depths, that wants to believe in a mechanical materialistic Universe, may on reflection, be the part of ourselves we want to determine our fate.*
>
> <u>*Know thyself, commanded the Sun god*</u>*. The techniques taught in ancient times in the Mystery schools and in modern times by groups like the Rosicrucians are intended to help us become aware of the rhythms of our breaths, our hearts, our sexual rhythms, the rhythm of waking, dreaming and dreamless sleep. If we can consciously attune our own individual rhythms to the rhythms of the cosmos measured by Jakin and Boaz*, it is suggested we may eventually join our individual evolutions with the evolution of the cosmos.*

> *This would be to find meaning in life in meaning's highest sense."* (**Jakin* means firm/upright/stable; *Boaz* is power or might.)

Our Otherworldliness, the Independent Events of our Emotions, is critical to our physical and mental health that has perhaps been Humanity's Quest all along? Namaste, Beautiful Souls.

Our Emotions connected to Source, sometimes gives us hints of Nature's Intent with just a small flip of sensations inside us that we can overlook if we are not paying attention. Every sensation has meaning. Tune-in to yourself, Beautiful Souls. **Richer I have become because I have learned How to Listen.**

3
LAW OF ACTION

FEAR inside our minds and bodies shut off our immune system. Yes—OFF completely. Fear puts our bodies in a state of flight or fight, and since the body cannot heal us at the same time, shuts down our immune system just like stress or fretting over depression. Beings CHOOSE whether to feel the stressor or not. But when it comes to flight or fight, the adrenaline rush is taken under the control of our Subconscious that also shuts OFF consciousness and takes over the self-preservation. Given that our hearts are 5,000 times more powerful than our minds, the Subconscious is our direct link to our hearts and God-Universe (Source).

LIES/DECEITS are everywhere but our build-in lie-detectors are also OFF. Humans are pre-programmed to take in all stimuli around us without prejudice and allowing time to pass before placing importance on things we experience or information we have heard. This is called information incubation, which is required for all new Knowledge. Everything energy in the Universe has an incubation timeframe before setting seed or manifesting.

HATE is an Emotion of our childishness that can be felt by young and old alike to protect our quantum self from harm. THIS Childishness is the inner faith that we can do anything! Childishness is best described by a song of music group, (YouTube) FEARLESS SOUL, called "Thoughts Become Things" and because its words ring TRUTH, I would like to share some with you—(It is probably best to hear the song for yourself on YouTube, search— FEARLESS SOUL music for song titled—

31

Thoughts Become Things

The 70,000-80,000 thoughts flashing through the mind are just a rolling scroll of noise. You can choose to merely watch every thought fly-by without emotionally reacting to any of the noise. Without reactions, the noise will eventually stop. Observer Beings—literally everything in the Universe is wavelengths/ energy. Everything about Humanity is energy— good or bad. As a whole I prefer to think of Humanity as good, but possibilities are not so cut and dry as that, because Egotism still exists. *"For I say, through the Grace given unto me, to every man that is among you, to think of himself more highly than he ought to think; but to think soberly**, according as God hath dealt to every man the measure of faith*."* (Romans 12:1-3)

*FAITH IN SELF and **Soberly to our
Emotions is meant as—Balance.

Every one of our Emotions has experienced the same as you, Observer Beings. Hence, your Emotions give you plenty of head noise that Science predicts some 70,000-80,000 thoughts per day. Balanced Emotions takes focus, Beautiful Souls. Balanced Emotions bring Peace, Joy, Truth and Unconditional Love with direct link to Source. To get through the inner focus needed to find Balance, you might cry and not yet know why? You may have words spill from your lips not knowing where they come from? You might have many experiences you cannot explain **while** you are experiencing them? Keep ASKING the right questions, Observer Beings because with FAITH in yourself, you can find the answers you are seeking, but all twelve Laws of the Universe should be followed to receive consistent Abundance available to Humanity. (See the 12 chapter Titles for the 12 Laws of the Universe work together in a harmonious rhythm within our Subconscious, which also has its own rhythms.

Next, let's consider five fractals of information.

1. Man's inherent desires for Ego-gratification
2. *"All things and events are foreshown and brought into being by causes; but the causation is of two Kinds: There are results originating from*

the Soul, and results due to other causes, those of the environment."
[Plotinus, <u>Ennead</u> 3.1.9]

3. The instability of the atom's ground from its core to a specific photon frequency—the Ego-Guilt emotion;
4. Teenage rebellion;
5. Adult reliance on (a) prescription and non-prescription drugs and (b) ideas of conceptualized Utopian Heavens.

The five items appear at first to be unrelated. I slept on them overnight to allow my brain time to process them and my emotions to consider possibilities. By combining points 4 and 5, I'm sure someone could probably come up with the concept, *'Teenage rebellion leads to adult drug reliance.'* Yet this possibility ignores the other three points. And I am sure a study could be done proving 4 and 5 are linked in some way, but again the others are ignored. Perhaps adding the others paints an ugly picture most people would probably choose to ignore in order to avoid discomfort? And they do.

Plotinus' first point, *results originating from the Soul*, refers to irresponsible Beings, and his second point, *environmental causes*, refers to adults who don't understand their role in teenage rebellion, thus bringing about adult reliance for counseling help from Dr. Phil. A third cause for teenage rebellion can arise from a combination of the two.

Adults inadvertently teach children to be socially-acceptable little robots, to fit-in, to keep up with friends, and to be part of the in-crowd. Why? Adults strive hard to fit-in and be part of the in-crowd, which is a fragment of a think-like-me dynamo. Adults learned from their parents and their parents before them, and so on. *"I" am the mother of my father and the sister of my husband, and he is my offspring.* [*The Nag Hammadi Library in English*, p 297] On the other hand, Adults like to teach youths to *think outside the box* because it enhances Creativity and builds intelligence. Yet they shake a stern finger at kids if outside-the-box thinking disrupts the precious structure for how adults feel things should be.

> *"I go along with the 5,000-year-old philosophy of the Bhagavad-Gita which says, "Action is the product of the qualities inherent in nature. It is only the ignorant man who,*

> *misled by personal egotism, says: 'I am the doer.'"* [*Utopia or Oblivion: the Prospects for Humanity*, p 12]

The desire for ego-gratification has permeated throughout History in the mind of humans for every little accomplishment. *"Nothing is so common as the wish to be remarkable."* [Shakespeare]. This addicts children to the highs of ego gratification along with its physical caustic effects of addiction to opiate-like endorphins. Adults attempt to teach children what is best for them based upon adult Life-Learned Lessons (LLLs) and proclaim, *"It is like trying to teach Geometry to a chicken."* Perhaps adult LLLs are outdated? Perhaps when a child reaches teenage years, rebellion occurs because innate-childlike sensibilities have been violated by outdated LLLs? In our fast changing times, since the Industrial Revolution began, experience can be our worst enemy.

Get Real

To claim to be a Chosen One, Knowing the Mysteries of the Deep, Ordained above all others Is a bunch of hooey.

In one's Delusions of Grandeur these concepts can come forth. But the only thing it proves is they are extreme Emotional Drunks.

To Proclaim that one is a Messiah is to expose they are psychotic. The only people to ever believe them are ones steeped in superstition.

The Goodness of our Religions, The Ignorance of our Prejudices, And the Passions of our Vanity Can all be hindrances to Realism.

While they seem to know a lot, this can be only relative. For as one's knowledge grows even greater becomes what they do not know.

34

We all are on a Journey, but be leery of what you think.
Do not try to fly too high without the Guidance of
Humility.

Why not instead teach *Being gratification*, the gratification coming from knowing we 'added a penny' to a greater project for humankind? Perhaps we can teach, "Be satisfied with Enough." It is the caustic Ego who tells us "I want it All," or "I know it All." Otherwise, by the time our youths reach puberty they have become know-it-alls and act like adults are ignorant. Perhaps rebellious teenagers are right? Since kids grow up addicted to the caustic effects of opiate-like endorphins, they eventually turn to drugs or seek answers within a cult that preaches of Utopia, which fulfills the addiction to the opiate-like endorphins—a never-ending cycle.

Perhaps atomic instability viewed by today's physicists is caused by instability of the atom's ground from the higher indigo frequency range of Ego-Guilt to its core, which then shows itself in rebellious teenagers and leads to reliance on pills in adults? All of this precludes adult personal responsibility to correct our brain wiring. Therefore, Plotinus was correct when he wrote, *"There are results originating from the Soul and results due to other causes, those of the environment."*

Be on your guard! [Aware]
Do not hate my obedience
and do not love my self-control.
In my weakness, do not forsake me,
    and do not be afraid of my power.
For why do you despise my fear
    and curse my pride?
But "I" am she who exists in all fears
    and strength in trembling.
    "I" am she who is weak [in the conscious mind],
and "I" am well in a pleasant place.
    "I" am senseless and "I" am wise [within the Subconscious].

Beings must use inspiration as motivation to action. Inspiration guarantees our motivation comes from the heart, which ties us directly to Source (God-Universe). The child in us used heart Inspiration for Creating, because <u>Thought plus Emotion equals Creation</u> for living our lives.

(THOUGHTS BECOME THINGS song by Fearless Soul, YouTube)

From an Elder Sioux teacher to children of the tribe:

> *"Take kindly as the council of the Earth gracefully SURROUNDING THE THINGS OF YOUTH. Nurture strength of spirit to shield you in sudden misfortune. Do not distress yourself with imaginings. Many fears are born in fatigue and loneliness, beyond the wholesome discipline. Be gentle with yourself. You are a child of the Universe. No less than the trees and the stars, you have a right to be here. And whether or not it's clear to you, no doubt the Universe is unfolding as it should. Be at peace with God whatever you conceive him to be. And whatever your labors and aspirations in the noisy confusion of life, keep peace with your Soul with all the shame, drudgery and broken dreams. It's still a beautiful world. Be cheerful and strive to be happy."*

Human's only limitations are weakness of focus/attention and shortage of imagination. Return to Childishness when you found something you absolutely loved doing from your heart. Creativity silences the mind.

4

LAW OF CORRESPONDENCE

An ancient Vedic expression can be sensed from the Subconscious mind—

> *"As in the microcosm, so is the macrocosm. As is the atom, so is the universe; as is the human body, so is the cosmic body. As is the human mind, so is the cosmic mind."*

I have experienced quite a few of these Subconscious functions—

- Silence of mind
- Involuntary and vegetation functions (*probably once I fully understand*)
- Informing Being of Nutrition, don't need anyone telling you what-to-EAT.
- Waste
- Cell waste
- Cell development
- Perceives by Intuition
- Extra-sensory perception (ESP)
- Power of inductive reasoning is perfection, from general to specific
- Reads thoughts of others
- Receives intelligence at a distant and then retransmits to others also at a distance

- Never dies
- Is your Soul and your personality
- Is a living Soul regardless of body entered into
- Is a work of assimilation
- Warns Beings of danger
- Approves/disapproves of the course of conduct in conversation and keeps a person in calm and quietness
- A master chemist, if Beings permit, if left to its own workings providing conscious mind doesn't change the course of its manifestation
- Carries out all ideas coming to it
- Keeps a body in health and vitality, if Being permits
- The most powerful force in Life and the most charitable—beneficent, Like a live WIRE
- Either your servant or your master; do you evil or do you good
- Is the subjective mind because it doesn't decide and command; it's motivated by what's in your heart
- A subject not a ruler, the Subconscious contains all the Knowledge and Wisdom of your current lifetime and past ages
- Our direct-link to God-Universe/Source
- We are all sons and daughters of God-Universe
- Never sleeps
- Takes over during duress—shutting off your conscious mind

As above, so below . . .

Functioning with properly balanced Emotions is not the end-game. The consummation of the age (after 2020 Winter Solstice) is a new beginning for our Universe (the Cosmic Mind). The son-of-man and 'True-Man' should be better prepared to explore what Nature has to offer.

> *"For everyone must go to the place from which he has come. Indeed, by his acts,* ('hands' in Revelations) *and his acquaintance* ('forehead' in Revelations) *each person will make his nature known."* [The Nag Hammadi Library, p 189]

"Shutting out all external sense objects, keeping the eyes and vision concentrated between the two eyebrows (pineal gland*), suspending the inward and outward breaths within the nostrils—thus controlling the mind, senses and intelligence, the transcendentalist becomes free from desire, fear and anger. One who is always in this state is certainly liberated."* [Bg. 5.27-28]

"The Blessed Lord [ATP] *said: He who does not hate illumination, attachment and delusion when they are present, nor longs for them when they disappear; who is seated like one unconcerned, being situated beyond these material reactions of the modes of nature, who remains firm, knowing that the modes alone are active; who regards alike pleasure and pain, and looks on a clod, a stone and a piece of gold with an equal eye; who is wise and holds praise and blame to be the same; who is unchanged in honor and dishonor, who treats friend and foe alike, who has abandoned all fruitive undertakings—such a man is said to have transcended the modes of nature."* [Bg. 14.22-25]

These three paragraphs are Nature's messages for balanced Emotions and Emotional Balance.

The Holy Grail of our physiological quest relates the description of four horse riders of the Book of Revelation to four chemicals in our brain. The Subconscious knows this, but the jumbled-up 70,000-80,000 thoughts in our heads makes it difficult to know much beyond conceptualized realities.

Dr. Deepak Chopra's important question:

"If many cells in our bodies are replaced every three months, then why do we still have the same illnesses?"

Dr. Chopra was spot-on with his answer:

"The answer I give is that through our own conditioning, we generate the same impulses of energy and information that lead not only to the same behavioral outcomes, but also lead

> *to the same biochemical processes, and that these biochemical*
> *processes are under the influence of our consciousness, our*
> *memory, and our conditioned responses."*

To get out of rigid-thinking rut, we must change our motivation from ego or sense gratification, i.e. feel-good endorphin highs. We must return our motivation to those of our younger Child, to our informative, inquisitive years <u>before we started learning how to just believe</u>, because it was easier than thinking for ourselves. The alternative to believing is to analyze EVERYTHING in terms of the probability of possibilities. Poker players do it all the time, called *pot-odds*. Another example would be to perceive all Life forms, including our own, in terms of our behavioral immune systems:

Behavioral (functions with Intent);
Immune (Self-preservation);
System (a complex Emergence).

Logically, all Life forms are a complex Emergence, functioning with Intent, and are devoted to Self-preservation—survival-of-the-fittest. Understanding Life requires examining its physical composition to grasp complexities involved in Emergence—the synergetic effects of combining energies, which some might refer to as Creation.

Scientists calculated the probability of success for how to put us on the moon long before the abominable feat was accomplished. Can the same be calculated for parallel universes as long as our conceptualized ideas about them are redefined as 'parallel realities' for 'True Man' to explore and develop? Herein lies the beauty of Nature's Unknown with words from England's Dr. Who character, *"The Quest is the Quest."*

("I" am) **iniquity** within.

("I" am) **truth** of the natures.

"I" am **the power** of the creation of the (spirits) [*the Gods*].

"I" come at the request of the soul [*all-encompassing of its parts that's parts much larger than mere Ego*].

"I" am control [*psychoses*] and the uncontrollable [*schizophrenia*].

"I" am the union and the dissolution.

"I" am the abiding and "I" am the dissolution.

"I" am the one below,

and they come up to me.

"I" am the judgment and the acquittal.

"I", "I" am sinless,

and the root of sin derives from me.

"I" am lust in outward appearance,

and interior self-control exists within me.

"I" am the hearing which is attainable to everyone

and the speech [*analog/gut feelings*]which cannot be grasped.

"I" am a mute who does not speak,

and great is my multitude of words.

5

LAW OF CAUSE AND EFFECT

"To sum the results of our argument: All things and events are foreshown and brought into being by causes. But the causation is of two Kinds; there are results originating from the Soul and results due to other causes, those of the environment. In the action of our Souls all that is done of their own motion in the light of sound reason is the Soul's work, while what is done where they are hindered from their own action is not so much done as suffered. <u>Unwisdom</u>, then, is not due to the Soul, and, in general—if we mean by Fate a compulsion outside ourselves—an act is fated when it is contrary to Wisdom. But all our best is of our own doing: such is our nature as long as we remain detached. The wise and good do perform acts; their right action is the expression of their own power: in the others it comes in the breathing spaces when the passions are in abeyance; but it is not that they draw this occasional Wisdom from outside themselves; simply, they are for the time being unhindered." [Ennead 3.1.9]

Science writer John Horgan wrote in his book <u>Rational Mysticism</u> [p 208],

"The forms shifted, tumbled, quivered, danced with a kind of mischievous intelligence. They were showing off, trying

to stagger me with increasingly ostentatious displays of otherworldly beauty." John recalled Terrence McKenna's similar descriptions of the entities he encountered, *"merry elfin, self-transforming machine creatures," "friendly fractal entities," "self-dribbling Faberge eggs on the rebound."*

Though Mr. Horgan's depiction of the Subconscious was accurate, he recalled looking for a revelation, but none came. Revelations don't seem to happen suddenly. Revelations slowly shift and evolve as the brain accommodates the reality of our Subconscious. This is when observations and perspectives about everything change. Day-to-day living becomes easier as the energies running our Universe sync-up with our body and act as guides through life's muddled maze. What energies? What am I talking about?

I am talking about Nature. I'm talking about the *quantum weirdness* physicists observe in their labs:

> *"The forms shifted, tumbled, quivered, danced with a kind of mischievous* **intelligence**. . . *trying to stagger me with increasingly ostentatious displays of otherworldly beauty."*

None of us want to know we've been wrong about nearly everything we have learned and had come to know about our lives—controversy? None of us want to know we do not control our thoughts, our day, our lives? Yet on the other hand, everyone wants cures for mental and physical ailments— *Our Physiological Quest*, the same since our humble beginnings. Due to the complexities within our Subconscious mind, it had been difficult to discern its actuality.

> *"They will object that parts must necessarily fall under one ideal-form with their wholes. And they will adduce Plato as expressing their view where, in demonstrating that the All is ensouled, he says—As our body is a portion of the body of the All, so our soul is a portion of the soul of the All."*
> [Ennead 4.3.1]

43

Probabilistic Terms

Regardless of race, oaths, or beliefs, the ancient Mayans predicted humankind will 'come together for One Cause'. Our future depends on it. Just the word—Apocalypse—can instill fear in our minds. But, with the plethora of Knowledge available to us now, what is there to fear in our 21st century? *Apocalypse* translates to 'lifted veil' that had begun after 2012. Ancient documents of the Nag Hammadi library refer to the veil covering our Subconscious mind as a "fleshly veil." But if anyone, besides secret-society initiates, has not experienced their Subconscious, then can the outcome of the experience be properly predicated?

> *"Our use of probabilistic terms to describe the outcome of events in everyday life is therefore a reflection not of the intrinsic nature of the process but only of our ignorance of certain aspects of it."* [Stephen Hawking, <u>The Grand Design</u>, p 74]

In other words, the answer to the above 'properly predicated' question is simply—No. After the *veil lifts* to our Subconscious when the numerous energies pour into our consciousness, humans are forced to know themselves in order to survive, fulfilling the prophecy of the Hopi Indian Prophecy Rock. The Hopi prediction describes two distinct paths for humans. One path is barren. The other is prolific and humans know themselves through finding their Authentic self with their Subconscious.

The Subconscious stirs the controversy pot to overflowing. Why? The reason is Universal Truths about our existence lie there, which is closer to Nature's Truths/Wisdom. The Truths/Wisdom about *our physiological quest* will appear approximately 170^0 away from where we should be to naturally heal what ails us. These Truths/Wisdom provide answers for Nature's flaw since *in the beginning*.

The keys to unlocking the mysteries of the universe and of Life lie with the understanding of the Subconscious, a natural occurring randomizer, with seven very mischievous Emotions, which are hidden. <u>Unless our Emotions are disciplined by the Gods, they are pathological liars</u> for what we consider 'real' while believing word thoughts. If they weren't liars,

44

scholars would have figured out the Universe long ago. The influences of our Emotions can be seen throughout the history of humans and our societies.

<u>Body is physical instrument. Subconscious is Energy-driver.</u>

> *"We make models in science, but we also make them in everyday life. Model-dependent realism applies not only to scientific models but also to the conscious and Subconscious mental models we all create in order to interpret and understand the everyday world. There is no way to remove the observer—us— from our perception of the world, which is created through our sensory processing and through the way we think and reason. Our perception—and hence the observations upon which our theories are based—is not direct, but rather is shaped by a kind of lens, the interpretive structure of our human brains."*
> [Stephen Hawking, <u>The Grand Design</u>, p 46]

Sometimes our Emotions get out of kilter. As a way for Nature to rebalance our neurotransmitters we are forced into a Low Energy State (LES) that we feel as depression. However, LES's, for the most part, do not have to be connected with depression or PTSD. Being calm yet alert, a good night's sleep, or relaxing are also examples of Lowest Energy States. Hence, LES's can be the preferred state to function most efficiently. The biggest threat to our brains achieving a LES is the release of adrenaline.

Depression is NOT A DIS-EASE!

A Law of Karma states, "What you resist persists." If a person resists depression, adrenaline is released in the body. A controlling neurotransmitter for adrenaline release is dopamine, which can be effected by our attitude. When combined with sensing a Need to cut adrenaline, we can also affect the release of GABA (a receptor blocker when learning anything new) resulting in a <u>simple one-two combination for whenever we need to 'chill-out.'</u> 1—you know you want to cut your adrenaline output and 2—Gamma-amino butyric acid (GABA) blocks all other receptors while its active.

Therefore, the important thing to remember is not to resist depression. Low Energy States are most useful when it comes to the mental function for predicating, thinking as opposed to doing physical labor or participating in athletic events, for instance. If you are a soldier in battle, you do not want to be in a LES!

Ms. *I-Wanna-Cry* Sadness, of our Creativity Emotion, may make us cry leaving us with a feeling of depression. However, depression has the effect of a Low Energy State in our brain and physical body. It is Nature's preferred, AND PERFECT, state to function, which is also how this book came to be written.

Low-Energy States can be sensed. Feeling internally calm, the feeling we have after a good night's sleep, or chilling-out are all examples of LESs So, why fight them? Feeling sloth-like is not a sin! It can also be during a period of an LES when the brain scrambles as a method of rebooting all of those fractals of information into a bigger picture, or as a method of balancing the effects of Divine energies manifesting themselves inside our brain and body.

Many times we confuse natural brain scrambling for periods of confusion (brain scrambling) which is then associated with more depression, causing domino effects of never-ending cycles. Fighting these sensations are the <u>main cause</u> of depression, anxiety, insomnia, and other emotional and physical ailments. Change motivations changes attitude about everything. Changing attitudes changes the mind. Change the mind—change the life.

The motivation for getting to know our self has to arise within the self, in particular from shifting motivation from ego gratification to Need of Childside, Resolve of the Mind, and Duty and Need of our Being. Attitude is vital when imbalances are looked upon as opportunities, as opposed to caustic responses from self-pity and complaining. Each of our paths will be as unique as our starting points and individual needs. Yet humans have left behind Nature and what can be learned from *Her.*

> *"The two processes, that of science and that of art, are not very different. Both science and art form in the course of the centuries a human language, by which we can speak about the more remote parts of reality . . ."*—Heisenberg, *Physics and Philosophy*

But *how* are Nature's laws enforced? Examining this question helps us understand *why* the 'Marriage' referred to in ancient texts and my friend's poetry involve Nature's attempt to permanently bond Existence and Intent.

The picture begins to take shape by combining ancient text, including the triangulation of The Thunder: Perfect Mind, The Book of Revelation, and the Bhagavad-Gita. The picture becomes clearer by adding fractals from other text, mix in modern science and an utterly beautiful masterpiece can begin to emerge.

> *"The higher the energy required to sustain a system, the less stable it is. Over time, an unstable system tends to settle back to its simplest lowest energy state: How long the process takes depends on the degree of instability."*—Roger Penrose, Discover, June, 2005 [p 33]

Mark Booth, author of *Secret History of the World,* warned of an Anti-Christ:

> *"Beware, too, of teaching that doesn't invite questioning, or tolerate mockery. It is telling you, in effect, that God wants you to be stupid."* [Secret History of the World, p 399]

Questioning everything is a healthy sign of an emerging Childside. As for mockery—well it will be welcome too; controversy sells. Controversy also means Nature is moving forward in Her quest to stabilize the atom—as All Knowledge is revealed at the End of Days.

Mark's statement, "God wants you to be stupid" is the same thing as saying, "The sum total of all energies everywhere wants any Being who clings to meaningless beliefs will remain stupid. Inspirational high-energy states are unstable and are expressed in our weakened immune system.

> *"We will regain some of the ability to control animals and plants by the power of our thoughts that Adam enjoyed."* [Secret History of the World, p 404]

- Was this statement from Mark Booth's brain-wiring, or analog messages he heard originating from the IOTC, which I Doubt?

- Wouldn't animals and plants have their own Mind, Awareness, and Intent controlling the providence of their lives?
- Why would they need mankind to do this for them?
- How do you know, Mark Booth, your own thoughts are not controlled? How do you know the book you wrote was the one *you* wanted to write?
- How do you know your emotions weren't interpreting messages from the IOTC as it opened up its flow of thought through your biologic internet?

"We will be aware of the spirits, then angels, and gods, alive in everything around us, but we will not be controlled by them anymore. We will become aware again of the spiritual beings ranged on either side of us whenever we make a decision." [Secret History of the World, p 404]

- How do you know, Mr. Booth, that your life has not been controlled all along?

> Be careful about clinging to delusions for controlling anything, arising from Egotism or egotistical brain wiring. It can be difficult for Beings to Let-Go of control along with addictions to endorphin highs. Survival demands turning control over to Nature. I know; I've been there. It is just as difficult for the Ego to let go of perceiving herself as *special* and *raising hell when she doesn't get her way*—the *Anti-Christ*, potentially existing within us all.

*Take me **to yourselves with*** *understanding from grief* [Lowest Energy State—LES, Nature's natural healing methodology to rebalance neurotransmitters].

> *and take me to yourselves from understanding (and) grief,*
> *And take me to yourselves from places that are ugly and in*
> *ruin* [our own emotions],

and rob from those which are good even though in ugliness.
Out of shame, take me to yourselves shamelessly;
and out of shamelessness and shame, upbraid my members
*   in yourselves.*
And come forward to me, you who know me
and you who know my members,
and establish the great ones [the four Horsemen of Revelations] *among the small first creatures* [Duty, Need, Childside & Resolve].
Come forward to childhood [child-like, inquisitive Childside in everyone],
and do not despise it because it is small and it is little,
And do not turn away greatnesses in some part from the smallnesses,
*   for the smallnesses* [New brain synapse formation, renewed Inspiration and Creativity]
are known from the greatnesses [increased intellect and healthier]

Adults are the models of society for children learning by watching and listening. But what can help channel Childside's orneriness earlier in children's lives? To provide Yin-Yang balance for Child's orneriness, perhaps Childside's fondness for <u>Resolve's reconnaissance missions</u> should be empowered? A definition of Emotional Balance was best provided in the Bhagavad-Gita.

"The Blessed Lord (ATP-brain messenger) *said: He who does not hate illumination, attachment and delusion when they are present, nor longs for them when they disappear; who is seated like one unconcerned, being situated beyond these material reactions of the modes of nature* (goodness, ignorance, passion), *who remains firm, knowing that the modes alone are active; who regards alike pleasure and pain, and looks on a clod, a stone and a piece of gold with an equal eye; who is <u>wise and holds praise and blame to be the same</u>; who is <u>unchanged in honor and dishonor</u>, who*

> *treats friend and foe alike, who has abandoned all fruitive undertakings—such a man is said to have* **transcended the modes of nature.**" [Bg. 14.22-25]

Much can be learned from Nature, such as how to naturally cure most of what ails us as long as we can get out of *Her* way. Nature can obsolete depression and PTSD as diseases: Mankind merely has to move away from the highs of sense gratification. I think I'll take my chance with adjusting to the **lowest** energy state of Nature. It has to be far better than the slow and agonizing die-off of the dinosaurs.

> *"Why do you* [Beings] *curse me ("I") and honor me? You have wounded and you have had mercy. Do not separate me from the first ones whom you have known."* [The Thunder: Perfect Mind]

Threats to Lowest Energy States

The biggest threat to our brains achieving a Lowest Energy State is the release of cortisol, which does not contain nitrogen. Cortisol can come with fighting depression, resulting in stress and anxiety. A controlling neurotransmitter for adrenaline release and other chemicals we can relate to feeling obsessed, such as cortisol, is dopamine. Dopamine can be affected by our attitude. When combined with the knowledge of our need to restrict obsession-based chemicals at times, we can also affect the release of GABA, a receptor blocker, resulting in a simple one-two combination for whenever we need to 'chill-out.'

If a person fights depression, cortisol is released in the body. Therefore, try not to fight depression. Instead, try to comprehend the basics of it to best handle each LES episode. We may not be able to tell when a person is in a depressive state, or Lowest Energy State, because of attitude. Some not only don't let the depression get them down, but can find pleasure it in while predicating an unresolved issue, which eventually arises to a satisfactory conclusion, hence a productive session.

With the proper attitude, depression can make us sensitive to what the Divine of our Subconscious are trying to communicate about ourselves. If done properly without the urge to fight what our Self is trying to do and tell us, Self-Esteem can emerge. Self-Esteem is the job of the Righteous emotion and her Humility. Righteous means whatever is right for our individuality. Humility is being humble without the need for Egotism bragging of our any accomplishments, as if the Ego had anything to do with ANY accomplishment of real value.

Getting Intune

The secret to sobering up our Emotions is getting in-tune with our controlling neurotransmitters. It is also important not to slip into self-pity, especially if sensing your Childside has surfaced. Sometimes, our emotions can also go on strike. For example, a caustic Ego stops telling us we are god-like, complicated by a contemptuous Guilt and scathing Obsession [adrenaline] pressuring us to get off our butts and start managing the world's affairs.

An example of a healthy attitude is to consider cleaning up our own house first. Try the LES of depression without caustic emotions sometime. You might find a totally different experience. I need to make a clear delineation between Guilt and Compunction—a feeling of inappropriateness for an action:

- "Those I Love, I chastise and rebuke—Compunction."
- "Those I wish to control and manipulate, I instill Guilt."

There are many advantages to properly predicating in LES's, with depression being only one LES example. If a person can get away from the influence of their caustic, unbalanced emotions as motivators, then perceptions will change for the better. Such is Nature.

A good night's sleep is a most invigorating Lowest Energy State.

6

LAW OF COMPENSATION

Egotism is unfathomable in its scope within brain-wiring. Egotism and vanity go DEEP. As one of the 'goddesses' to aid the Ego Emotion—sensed as Patience—can be beckoned into our Awareness to ignore brain-wired Egotism. Whether egotism is your motivation or brain-wired egotism comes back from memories, it is still about 180^0 out of phase with Nature and THE reason for devastating illnesses and disease. Brain-wired egotism and vanity can be subtle and difficult to recognize in your Self. *"Be on your guard!"* says the "I"

The following paragraph from The Nag Hammadi Library in English, pp 299-300, illustrates opposites in opinion between Egotism and functioning with the Subconscious mind.

"Why have you [Beings] *hated me in your counsels?*
For "I" shall be silent among those who are silent,
 and "I" shall appear and speak.
Why then have you hated me, you Greeks?
Because "I" am a barbarian among (the) barbarians?
For "I" am the wisdom (of the) Greeks
 and the knowledge of the barbarians.
"I" am the judgment of (the) Greeks and of the barbarians.
("I") am the one whose image [Ego/vanity motivated] *is great in Egypt and the*
 one who has no image [due to analog sensations] *among the barbarians.*
"I" am the one who has been hated everywhere
 and who has been loved everywhere.

"I" am the one whom they call Life,
  and you have called Death.
"I" am the one whom they call Law,
  and you have called Lawlessness.
    "I" am the one whom you have pursued [Ideas],
      and "I" am the one whom you have seized.
"I" am the one whom you have scattered,
  and you have gathered me together [Ideas].
"I" am the one before whom you have been ashamed,
  and you have been shameless to me.
"I" am she who does not keep festival,
  and "I" am she whose festivals are many.
    "I", "I" am godless,
      and "I" am the one whose God [The Infinite/Intent] *is great.*
    "I" am the one whom you have reflected upon [as a 'God'],
and you have scorned me [the Subconscious mind].
"I" am unlearned,
  and they learn from me.

[The Mirror of the Self]

"I" am the one whom you have despised,
  and you reflect upon me.
"I" am the one whom you have hidden from,
  and you appear to me.
But whenever you hide yourselves,
"I" myself will appear.
For whenever you appear,
  "I" myself will hide from you.
Those who have **_appeared_** *to it* **_hide_** *senselessly* **_from it_**
  (the "I"—the Subconscious mind).

Our mind and the hydrogen atom need balance with Nature. No magic pill will fix the current imbalance. It has to come from within. We can only listen to ourselves throughout each day. Take inventory. Where do our motivations lie? Why do some people irritate us and others do not?

How do we know when we have found ourselves, our purpose, and the meaning to life?

> *"Thus the universal circuit* (IOTC) *would seem to be the monarch of the All. Now a first answer to this theory is that its advocates have merely devised another shift to immolate* [sacrifice] *to the heavenly bodies all that is ours, our acts of will and our states, all the evil in us, our entire personality; <u>nothing is allowed to us</u>; we are left to be stones set rolling, not men, not beings whose nature implies a task. . . . <u>A further confirmation is found in the efforts we make to correct both bodily constitution and mental aspirations.</u>"* [Ennead 3.1.5]

The doorway to our Subconscious is like entering a website on the internet and once there, a person is opened up to a whole new *multi-dimensional* internet. We are knocking on its door when we monitor our gut feelings, or do something creative with our hands causing our biologic brain to shut-off word thoughts. These simple practices are what Sorcerer, Yaqui shaman don Juan Matus (written about by Carlos Castaneda's) would refer to as shifting our assemblage point from our *conditioned, external perceived believed world reality* to the internal part of perception in the realm of the unknown. Castaneda often referred to this unknown realm as non-ordinary reality, and it was indeed a reality, but fundamentally different from the *perceived world reality* currently experienced by humankind.

> *"Allow the cosmic circuit its part, a very powerful influence upon the thing brought into being: allow the stars a wide material action upon the bodily part of the man, producing heat and cold and their natural resultants in the physical constitution; still does such action explain character, vocation and especially all that seems quite independent of material elements, a man taking to letters, to geometry, to gambling, and becoming an originator in any of these pursuits? And can we imagine the stars, divine beings, bestowing wickedness?"* [Ennead 3.1.6]

Why do you [Beings] *curse me and honor me?*
You have wounded and you have had mercy.
Do not separate me from the first ones [4 Horsemen of Revelations] *whom*
  you have (known).
(And) do not cast anyone (out nor) turn anyone away
should they *turn you away and* **they** *(know) him not.*
  Know him. [Electron-field Wavefunction aka our Awareness]
  What is mine **is his** [Virtual photons—Emotions
  surrounding electrons].
  "I" know the first ones [—*Childside, Resolve, Duty, Need*]
  and those after them (know) me. (The Thunder: Perfect Mind)

The keys to unlocking the mysteries of the universe and of Life lie with understanding the Subconscious, a natural occurring randomizer, with seven very mischievous Emotions. Unless our Emotions are disciplined by Nature, Laws of the Universe and our Observer Being they are pathological liars that we consider 'real' when we believe our word thoughts. If they weren't, scholars would have figured out the universe long ago. The influences of our Emotions can be seen throughout the history of humans and our societies, answering the age-old questions about who I am and what is my purpose; focusing inward is the way to world peace.

Why? How? Do our know-it-all Egos avoid asking questions? Freud conceptualized the Ego, Id and Super Id, thinking they were a revelation, he didn't question anything else. His Ego had convinced himself he was a god. No Ego is totally accepting. No Ego is tolerant. Hanging on to the Ego is mostly irritating. Mostly, Egotists are offensive. And the ego can be as subtle as thinking someone stole your lunch money to boastful bragging and complaining.

People cling to their beliefs until their realities are stifled from actualities indicated by rising divorce rates, murders, riots, depression, suicides, sickness, child-cancers, and annoying pharmaceutical advertisements on the tele. Couldn't this be the reason PTSD hits so hard when traumatic events darken our lives? Or depression is made into a disease because nobody questions Nature's natural system for balancing our neurotransmitters?

"Embracing uncertainty does not mean that we stop searching
for solutions. It only means that we remind ourselves and each

other that our explanations are often based on insufficient understanding. Keeping cognizant of our own uncertainty empowers us to qualify our claims and moderate the solutions we adopt. Even more, it forces us to keep an open mind when we confront complex conditions. Open-minded sounds simple enough, but . . . it is how hard being open-minded really is." [Blunder, Why Smart People Make Bad Decisions, by Zachary Shore, p 231]

All of life (man, animal, or plant) is composed of physical bodies and a separate soul of EMR (electromagnetic radiation) that is throughout the body. You are not only whatever you eat, but you are what you think. Therefore, be cautious of whatever you believe within your word thoughts. Word thoughts can be, *electronically speaking*, electrical echoes bouncing off the wet atmosphere of our brain wiring. Thoughts should be ignored at first until the mind goes quiet. Only then, can a person hear Nature's music.

If Sensed, Then It IS Reality

Knowledge is knowledge and should never be incorrect. Either we know or we don't know. Today's public is bombarded with conflict among our scholars, which is like squabbling married couples airing dirty laundry for the whole neighborhood to hear and see.

"The two processes, that of science and that of art [religion], *are not very different. Both science and art form in the course of the centuries a human language by which we can speak about the more remote parts of reality . . ."* —Heisenberg, Physics and Philosophy

Let's consider the more remote parts of reality like angels, demons, and divine revealers. They all carry with them touches of mysticism and intrigue. Their identities have changed through the ages only in name.

- Have their mysterious secrets been hard-wired into our brains?
- Are they mere figments of our imaginations?

- Can their existence be reality inside the secret realm of our Subconscious mind?
- From where else can they arise?
- Given our brain can process eleven million bits-per-second [bps], why would Nature make our conscious mind so inefficient to process a mere 200 bps?
- Therefore, aren't beliefs of 'the divine' mere inspiring manifestations of our biological senses?
- We all have to believe in something, right?
- Or do we?

The observations of *Great Minds* throughout history have explained how conflict leading to consensus is inherent in the Nature of our Universe, our minds/Intellect, and our bodies. More importantly, these minds have used the eye of their mind to see the vision for everything in existence as being a smaller part of a much larger picture, even for our own Intellect.

> *"We may thus distinguish two phases of Intellect, in one of which it may be taken as having no contact whatever with particulars and no Act upon anything; thus it is kept apart from being a particular intellect. . . . The specific sciences lie in potentiality in science-the-total; even in their specific character they are potentially the whole; they have the whole predicated of them and not merely a part of the whole. At the same time, science must exist as a thing in itself, unharmed by its divisions. So with Intellect. Intellect as a whole must be thought of as prior to the intellects actualized as individuals; but when we come to the particular intellects, we find that what subsists in the particulars must be maintained from the totality. The Intellect subsisting in the totality is a provider for the particular intellects, is the potentiality of them: it involves them as members of its universality, while they in turn involve the universal Intellect in their particularity, just as the particular science involves science-the-total."*
> [Ennead 6.2.20]

As science delves deeper to uncover mysteries unknowable to our ancient ancestors, supplementary bits of our belief systems fall into the shadows of human memory. What science can exist where there is no order? Yet how can science progress past today's confusing and tumultuous times if it is to be left behind in the evolutionary dust by 'sticking to their guns'? Have we forgotten Milton's words from his Areopagitica:

> *"Where there is much desire to learn, there of necessity will be much arguing, much writing, many opinions; for opinion in good men is but knowledge in the making."* Aren't the Sciences expected to embrace conflict for the betterment of humankind instead of merely working for their own self-interest?

> *"We can in conclusion observe one obvious measure of the importance of being in philosophical thought. The major 'isms' by which the historians of philosophy have tried to classify its doctrines represent affirmations or denials with respect to being or the modes of being. They are such antitheses as realism and idealism; materialism and spiritualism; monism, dualism, and pluralism; even atheism and theism. Undoubtedly, no great philosopher can be so simply boxed. Yet the opposing isms do indicate the great speculative issues which no mind can avoid if it pursues the truth or seeks the ultimate principles of good and evil."* [Encyclopedia Britannica's "The Great Books of the Western World, Syntopicon I" p 109]

> *And do not banish me from your sight. And do not make your voice hate me, nor your hearing. Do not be ignorant of me anywhere or any time.* ***Be on your guard!*** [The Thunder: Perfect Mind]

Are We Mortals or Immortals?

When the author of *The Thunder: Perfect Mind* wrote *"and many are her sons"*, the featured segment of this chapter, 'sons' is symbolic of

immortal Beings: Life does not become mortal, of a set duration, until the soul enters a physical living body. Then, the soul's <u>physical</u> lifeline clock begins ticking down to death.

> *"Thereupon since the rulers* [there could be many lurking in the Infinite] were envious of Adam [the atom] *they wanted to diminish their* [souls] *lifespans. They could not because of fate [the laws of physics], which had been fixed since the beginning. For to each had been allotted a lifespan of 1,000 years according to the course of the luminous bodies. But although the rulers could not do this, each of the evil doers took away ten years. And all this lifespan which remained amounted to 930 years* [insinuates our 7 emotions to be the cause]: *and these are in pain and weakness and evil distraction. And so life has turned out to be, from that day until the consummation of the age."* [Nag Hammadi Library in English, On the Origin of the World, p 185]

> *"By human calculation, a thousand ages taken together is the duration of Brahma's* [the indestructible, transcendental living entity's] *day. And such also is the duration of his night."* [Bg. 8.17]

Perhaps the Bhagavad-Gita and On the Origin of the World were written around the same timeframe? Or perhaps not? Nonetheless, Hindus believe burning the physical body after death prevents the invisible soul from re-entry into another body. Are they attempting to cheat fate? OR does our energy-efficient Universe prevent cheating from happening?

Vision vs. Contemplation

> *"We must admit that the Soul before entering into birth presents itself bearing with it something of its own, for it could never touch body except under stress of a powerful inner impulse* [Perhaps the pineal gland's magnetic particle arrangements are like snowflakes, different in everyone?];

> *we must admit some element of chance around it from its*
> *very entry, since the moment and conditions are determined*
> *by the Cosmic Circuit."* [Ennead 2.4.10]

It is difficult to know where our soul came from before entering our body. Neither do we know whether the nuclear generator of our soul, our Being, is nearing the end of its consummation. Perhaps the 930 years was merely an approximation for how long higher-energy states can be sustained before the atom returns to its original form, broken apart to return to the 'Infinites' of pure energy? Can these infinites be the background noise observed by today's physicists, reminding us of our Purpose—survival?

The Childside of Plotinus, (205-270AD)

> *"Supposing we played a little before entering upon our serious*
> *concern, and maintained that all things are striving after*
> *Contemplation, looking to Vision as their one end—and*
> *this, not merely Beings endowed with reason, but even the*
> *unreasoning animals, the Principle that rules in growing*
> *things, and the Earth that produces these—and that all*
> *achieve their purpose in the measure possible to their kind,*
> *each attaining Vision and possessing itself of the End in its*
> *own way and degree, some things in entire reality, others in*
> *mimicry and in image—we would scarcely find anyone to*
> *endure so strange a thesis. But in a discussion entirely among*
> *ourselves there is no risk in a light handling of our own ideas."*
> [Ennead 3.8.1]

Plotinus was in a playful mindset with his words and with the very philosophical points he was sharing. The message he felt in his gut to transcribe into digital words made him feel a little giddy—child-like.

> *"Well—in the play of this very moment am I engaged in*
> *the act of Contemplation? Yes; I and all that enter this play*
> *are in Contemplation: our play aims at Vision; and there is*
> *every reason to believe that child or man, in sport or earnest,*

is playing or working only towards Vision, that every act is an effort towards Vision; the compulsory act, which tends rather to bring the Vision down to outward things, and the act thought of as voluntary, less concerned with the outer, originate alike in the effort towards Vision." [Ennead 3.8.1 cont'd]

7

LAW OF ATTRACTION

Likes Attract Likes, period. Are you vibrating with Emotions you want to attract? Are you incorporating all the Laws of the Universe in your every-day contemplations? If you ponder any fears which may be bestowed upon us through inner turmoil caused by external stimulus, you can begin to see that these fears are not necessarily real or justified. Fear is mostly a lack of knowledge about something or someone and the lack of Knowledge increases adrenaline in the body as well as the negative effects of adrenaline and cortisol. For these reasons, gaining Knowledge throughout life is crucial to healthy brain functions.

Nonetheless, ponder this question, "Why do we want to destroy, bury or hide that which we do not understand? If you don't think that humans do this, then look at this short list of fears I wrote down in less than ten minutes. FEAR OF:

1. Becoming like mother/father
2. Darkness
3. Public Speaking
4. Death
5. Success
6. Change
7. Losing Control
8. Speaking up and facing ridicule
9. Failure

10. Suffering
11. Losing our innocence—something about our inner child
12. Never being able to know our Authentic self
13. Never being able to understand why we function
14. Etcetera, etcetera . . .

<u>The Great Books of the Western World</u> on the subject of Emotions, *"The emotions claim our attention in two ways. We experience them, sometimes in a manner which overwhelms us; and we analyze their role in human life and society. We seldom do both at once, for analysis requires emotional detachment, and moments of passion do not permit study or reflection . . ."* Why were you born? What purpose do you have in walking this planet? Do you want to function efficiently without undue anxiety or stress or depression? The only way to achieve this is to separate your afflicted self from your Authentic self. Incorrect beliefs about yourself can act as shackles for your Subconscious energies that are affecting your body. Shackles can cause undue fears or could be the actual fears.

I know emotional shackles as the things which cause fears or the shackles could be the fears themselves. There is nothing in this world that can actually control our internal freedoms. This freedom is what you want to seek in order to help find your Authentic self. You can choose, Dear Beings, who puts shackles on you and your Emotions.

> *"Emotional experience seems to involve an awareness of widespread bodily commotion, which includes changes in the tension of the blood vessels and the muscles, changes in heartbeat and breathing, changes in the condition of the skin and other tissues. Though some degree of bodily disturbance would seem to be an essential ingredient in all emotional experience, the intensity and extent of the physiological reverberation, or bodily commotion is not the same or equal in all the emotions. Some emotions are much more violent than others . . ."* (Encyclopedia Britannica on 'Emotion')

Imagine reality full of 'Spock' humans like in Star Trek. No Vanity. No Ego. No control. No Emotional outbursts. No Egotism. No

Guilt. No Shackles. Without Egotism hijacking the other Emotions, neurotransmitters fire normal. Sickness fades as bacteria die. Without Egotism, self-righteousness evaporates along with desires, praise and recognition for efforts. Depression is embraced as Nature's methodology to balance the neurotransmitters. Dread and Sloth are hugged as Nature's ways to relax and predicate the ways of the Universe. Creativity, Love and Wisdom flourish throughout the Universe.

> *"Knowledge is the amassed thought and experience of innumerable minds."*—Ralph Waldo Emerson

Rene Descartes recommended that we see the bigger picture. The bigger picture of our Subconscious is best expressed from the ancient **Vedic** expression:

> **"As in the microcosm, so is the macrocosm. As is the atom, so is the universe; as is the human body, so is the cosmic body. As is the human mind, so is the cosmic mind."**

8

LAW OF PERPETUAL TRANSMUTATION OF ENERGY

My friend, Ronald Grafton, had written a story about mental constructs that can wonderful by using Harvard physicist, Lisa Randall, who he things is beautiful. His construct was that she is his girlfriend and is his most wonderful construct ever. He went through a large list of arguments but none of them hold up to reality, which is the point for all mental constructs. He says mental constructs shouldn't have to stand up to reality because they are 'beautiful just the way they are'. I would add that they can be healthy if Beings choose to function with them in the 4th Dimension-higher vibration of Dream-states while they are LETTING THEM GO.

Always remember that mental images are energy. Remember your concepts or constructs, whatever you wish to call them, become matter once you also apply Emotion to them. Realize you have the power to do that; knowing what you want first would be most helpful. Once you know what you want, then focus thought and Emotion on the image of your desires with single-minded purpose.

Defining truth and an ancient healing science for Hindus are the **Vedas**, which are the most ancient religious texts. They got their present form between 1200-200 BCE and were introduced to India by the Aryans. Hindus believe that the texts were received by scholars direct from God and passed on to the next generations by word of mouth.

Vedas describe such universal truths: Soul Theory, yoga, yogic meditation, yogic powers, reincarnation, destiny, birth-maturity-death of all objects, eternal recurrence, memory in the nature, etc. All of the modern religions, including Bible, Judaism, etc. describe them also. There was a time when Vedas were known all over the world.

Universal Truths of our Ancestors—*We are our Ancestors*

1. You are exactly where you are supposed to be
2. Fear and pain are life's greatest teachers
3. Laughter and play are the keys to the fountain of youth
4. Exercise and rest are the keys to vibrant health
5. Touch and intimacy are basic human needs
6. Everything is impermanent
7. Everything is connected

Cosmic Actualities from the Subconscious Energies

1. The Intent of any creation, our Universe included, is for the entertainment of the energies of Potentiality involved; or simply "something to do."
2. Any Reality is but an Illusion.
3. We are made of quantum-zoo capable atoms: If you experience something, *then it must exist.*
4. The Actuality is the Actuality, or simply A equals A.
5. If you cannot control something to a degree of 100%, then it must be regarded as an Independent Event.
6. There is only NOW: *Being in the Present state of flow.*
7. We don't have to know it all or have proof in order to function in the Subconscious realm with its Divinity.

The Hopi Indian Prophecy Rock holds the Truth: Either know thyself and crops flourish. OR ignore Nature's shove toward Humanity's evolutionary Phase Shift—crops die and life dies. WARNING—EVERYTHING IS CONNECTED. Nature's influence spilling quantum realities into our own has been underway since the Battle of Bastogne, December, 1944, creating chaos, hate, discontent and death. CLUE—the energies of our

Subconscious minds are here and now introducing themselves whether mankind is prepared or NOT! It's better to get prepared than to lose all Hope of regaining sanity and making true breakthroughs.

The results for me included a new stronger immune system, individuality, balanced Emotions and a silenced mind. Stillness. Peaceful. Calm. While conscious minds can process a mere 40 bps; research has shown the Subconscious mind can process 40 million bps. At that speed, I observe everything, taking it ALL in without emotional prejudice. *With or without my Awareness* I send everything off to 'Sara' (Serotonin, our inner *Counselor,* same for our Emotions). The Cosmos and my Emotions process the result. Some time may pass before I receive a potential solution— usually brilliance coming from the Cosmos. Timing is everything. I don't hurry or obsess anything. Emotional Emotions happening to you are transpired by you—Being-Observer. Are you and your Ego addicted to endorphin highs?

The Breakthrough Round Tables have no room for Egotism or vanity Highs. Just read Ecclesiastes—everything is vanity. Most religions groom egotism and vanity to attract and control the masses, killing individuality and making people irresponsible for their own actions by spewing a few halleluiahs and Hail Mary's. Halleluiahs and pedestals do not make a difference in our health except to make us sick.

> *"We may become less quick to presume that our intuitions, our brilliant ideas are our own—and more open to the suggestion that they might be otherworldly promptings. As well as becoming aware that we may be prompted by disembodied intelligence, we may realize, too, that we are connected with one another more directly through thinking than we are through speech and physical observation."* The Secret History of the World as laid down by the Secret Societies, Mark Booth,2008, The Overlook Press, pp 399-400.

Energies, don't stress over common constructs, therefore let's clear the slate:

1. EMR (electromagnetic radiation) is the "I" manifested as our Subconscious—not the villain in our realities. *The Book of Ecclesiastes is evolved around the villain.*

2. Humans have never nor will ever control anything. *If you cannot control something 100%, then it is an Independent Event.* Our 7 Emotions are Independent Events, or else our *word-thoughts* INTERPRETERS would be easy to control and **SHUT-OFF**.

3. Depression is Nature's system specifically to rebalance neurotransmitters. **EMBRACE IT—DO NOT RESIST IT.**

4. Hardening the brain, Believing anything not actual causes Alzheimer's. Our brain is intended to be a predicating brain. Faith is different given it is a useful **SHORT-TERM** temporary-home method of learning.

5. We are NOT biochemical machines controlled by genes. (*Implying we are without a soul?*) Magnetic particles in our pineal gland and bodies of 90% water is a most energy-efficient receiving antenna in existence. Our bodies are vessels for this life for which we should appreciate. After death, the soul sheds this physical body and moves on to the next body *when time is right.* (This attitude, activating dopamine, should lessen the Fear of Death.)

6. Ego if I'm Wrong: Guilt if I'm Right! *Ego **and** Judgment, both of the Mind, have no heart.* Cherry-picking data done by a few Academics is a sign of Egotism's *Last Stand.* Egotism dies with the Quantum Shift. *Hello Spock minds!*

Einstein was the first to refer to the atom's *spookiness*—We are made of them. Identical spookiness and/or *orneriness* can be experienced from the energies of the Subconscious, but the Subconscious consists of a specific *quantum zoo.* To avoid falling victim to the tricks and treacherous of the "I", source of the mind, ignore all word thoughts during the quantum shift because this female Dimension* of the Cosmos will use word thoughts and brain-wiring against everyone to accomplish her Intent. (Ever lost your car keys only to find them where you left them last? THAT IS the cause of the "I") It is best in the quantum Subconscious reality to <u>stay Aware without thinking</u>. Thinking is only thoughts and voices, UNLESS directly acted upon.

*A quantum Dimension is defined as ENERGY:

> *"Every piece of a dynamical system that can move independently is another variable, another degree of freedom. Every degree of freedom requires another dimension in phase space, to make sure that a single point contains enough information to determine the state of the system uniquely."* Gleick, James. <u>Chaos, Making a New Science</u>. Penguin Books. 1988. page 135

*Likewise, the "I" is capable of digital and analog communications.

9

LAW OF POLARITY, OF OPPOSITES OR MENTAL VIBES

Everything within has opposition (as resistance or conflict), and convergence (as in coming together and consensus); YIN is the masculine, such as male references to the Lord while YANG is the feminine, such as the female softer and kinder references for the Christ. Polarity in everything throughout the Universe allows us to re-evaluate perceptions.

> Perception is *"the process whereby Sensory Stimulation is translated into <u>organized or meaningful</u> Experience. The perceptual process is <u>not directly observable</u>, but relations can be found between the various <u>types of stimulation</u> and their associated experiences or percepts. Empirical (first-hand) demonstration of the difference between **sensation and perception** has been a classical problem largely because of a lack of agreement about the definition of the two terms. A common distinction is that sensations are simple sensory experiences while percepts are complex constructions of simple elements that have been joined through association . . ."* (Encyclopedia Britannica)

In re-evaluating perceptions, humanity is Being asked to break out of antiquated-structure concepts that make-up their current reality.

Breaking-out makes it easier to start looking at their sensory experiences from a different light.

> *"The point is that when it comes to the biggest questions, people are again not necessarily choosing according to the balance of the probabilities, which may be almost too small to measure. The world is like the 'perspected' picture that can equally well be seen as a witch or a pretty girl. People often choose one world-view in preference to another because somewhere in the depths of their Being that is what they WANT to believe. If we can become aware of this predisposition, we can make a decision which is—to that extent—free, because it is a decision based on knowledge. The part of us, somewhere in our depths, that wants to believe in a mechanical materialistic Universe, may on reflection, be the part of ourselves we want to determine our fate."*

> <u>*Know thyself, commanded the Sun god.*</u> *The techniques taught in ancient times in the Mystery schools and in modern times by groups like the Rosicrucians are intended to help us become aware of the rhythms of our breaths, our hearts, our sexual rhythms, the rhythm of waking, dreaming and dreamless sleep. If we can consciously attune our own individual rhythms to the rhythms of the cosmos measured by Jakin and Boaz* (known as opposites like in the 12 Laws of the Universe), *it is suggested we may eventually join our individual evolutions with the evolution of the cosmos. This would be to find meaning in life in meaning's highest sense."*

* *

My friend, Ronald, has his own relationship with ATP (see Scientific American April 2004, Other Half of the Brain.) I sense a similar relationship to a warrior sensation in ATP with internal Duty and Need, both arising from our fast-spinning graviton Being, which are easier to sense when in lower energy states. Additionally, the Bhagavad Gita could become the core basis of treating depression because it prepares warriors for battle. It has to do with Attitude Adjustments that triggers dopamine in the brain. It has to do with Duty and Need. After Arjuna (the Being) fell into shock over the impending war battle, Krishna (the Lord) predicated him out of it. This can establish how suffering minds can be **re-centered** after facing combat fatigue.

Yin-Yang balance is needed in our thinking to maintain elasticity in our uncertain, unpredictable future, a future potentially fraught with chaos as our galaxy realigns its electromagnetic forces. In the same way, Yin-Yang balance is needed to avoid structured brain-wiring, to build brain elasticity. Perhaps Nature's fury occurs for us to appreciate Nature's beauty, or perhaps it is motivation to create new beauty?

"As is the human mind, the microcosm, the atom, and the human body, so is the cosmic mind, the macrocosm, the universe, and the cosmic body." Eastern medicine runs on energy flow. Western medicine runs on snapshots. In times of natural disaster where human causalities are apparent, then doctors rely on the triage method of diagnosis based on functions, limits, and values (calculus), to see a bigger picture of the situation.

Triage is a system of assigning priorities, the probability of possibilities for success. East meets West during their finest hour of triage without realizing they both observe quality and quantity to save the most lives possible. *'But this body is not a husk having no part in soul . . . .'* An East-meets-West paradigm brings evidence to the table of the energy flow of our mind cannot be separate from body energy. *"As is the human body, so is the cosmic body."*

Cosmologists calculate our moon was closer to us in ancient times, given it is moving away from us an inch or so a year. Shouldn't the reason for the movement include the microcosm of our Universe? Open any physics book and a section on decay can be found.

- If the atom is losing electromagnetism, then isn't electromagnetism weakening throughout the Universe?
- Can a force of nature be calculated to better explain why our moon distancing itself from our planet?
- Could substituting the word 'entanglement' for 'inflation' help further define our existence?

> *"A living thing comes into existence containing Soul, present to it from the Authentic, and by Soul is inbound with Reality entire; it possesses also a body; but this body is not a husk having no part in Soul, not a thing that earlier lay away in the soulless; the body had its aptitude and by this draws near: now it is not body merely, but living body. By this neighboring it enhances with some impress of soul—not in the sense of a portion of soul entering into it, but that it is warmed and lit* (lit by light/photons-our Emotions) *by Soul entire: at once there is the ground of desire, pleasure, pain; the body of the living form that has come to be was certainly no unrelated thing."* [*Ennead 6.4.15]*by Plotinus (205-270AD)

Scientists observe an acceleration of Universe expansion, of heavenly bodies moving apart. An acceleration of decay should also be observable within the atom. An acceleration of decay should also become visible from data collected from the World Health Organization. Similar decay accelerations should be observable by the World Religious Order. If the acceleration continues, then won't we actually lose our moon, our health, and our minds? Answers lie in recognizing first and foremost, the components of the fundamental hydrogen atom are **Mind, Being, Awareness, and Intent** as the Enforcer of Nature's Universal Laws that stretch beyond the laws of Physics.

10

LAW OF RELATIVITY

From (<u>The Secret of the World as laid down by the Secret Societies</u>, Mark Booth, 2008, The Overlook Press, p 400—

"When it comes to contemplating such far-flung events as the beginning of the Universe, it is inevitable that huge amounts of speculation are mapped on to the smallest conceivable specks of evidence. Leading physicists', cosmologists' and philosophers' speculations on infinite interlocking dimensions, parallel universes and 'soap-bubble universes' involve just as much imagination as Aquinas's speculations about angels on a pinhead.

The point is that when it comes to the biggest questions, people are again not necessarily choosing according to the balance of the probabilities, which may be almost too small to measure. The world is like the 'perspected' picture that can equally well be seen as a witch or a pretty girl. People often choose one world-view in preference to another because somewhere in the depths of their Being that is what they WANT to believe. If we can become aware of this predisposition, we can make a decision which is— to that extent—free, because it is a decision based on knowledge. The part of us, somewhere in our depths, that wants to believe in a mechanical materialistic Universe, may on reflection, be the part of ourselves we want to determine our fate.

> *Know thyself, commanded the Sun god. The techniques taught in ancient times in the Mystery schools and in modern times by groups like the Rosicrucians are intended to help us become aware of the rhythms of our breaths, our hearts, our sexual rhythms, the rhythm of waking, dreaming and dreamless sleep. If we can consciously attune our own individual rhythms to the rhythms of the cosmos measured by Jakim and Boaz, it is suggested we may eventually join our individual evolutions with the evolution of the cosmos. This would be to find meaning in life in meaning's highest sense."*

Atoms and particles can act like waves; exhibiting waves-of-energy behavior whenever physicists run two-slit experiments on them. Yet, physicists sometimes describe atoms as particles consisting of structured pieces when using detectors to look at them. Misinterpreting these itty bitty snapshots of a Universe in motion ignores energies revealing themselves as intelligent and individualist waves functioning with Intent, similar to our Emotions. These and other energies, the Dimensions, arise from the atoms. We are physically made from atoms. Functioning with the Dimension of Intent gave rise to Life. These Dimensions have Intelligence because, **"How can the intelligence demonstrated in our mind arise from combining atoms unless intelligence is a fundamental part of the hydrogen atoms from which we are made?"**

Try answering this question without invoking *somehow-miraculously arising* Virgin Birth concepts or ignoring QED. Biological research has shown the photon displays intelligence by using its superposition capability (*being in more than one place simultaneously*) to find the most efficient method to enter a plant during photosynthesis. For years physicists have also seen intelligence demonstrated in atomic experiments.

Delving deeper, **"What gave rise to the energies of the atom from pure energy other than the unknown we can refer to as Intent."** When considering the amount of energy contained in a single hydrogen atom, Intent must be a very powerful enforcer, unlike conceptualized gods or mathematical formulae.

Using a logical thought process for the two boldfaced questions above can alter perspectives of Life and our universe, such as concluding

Intelligence and Intent were the **cause** for the onset of the universe. Another possibility could be the mind of humankind, all of life, the planets, our galaxy, and the Universe arose from electromagnetism inherent in the atom.

When Creativity is active, the neurotransmitter *Glutamate* is at work, the most prevalent in the brain and is produced by the body! Active glutamate is the only chemical the body uses to prevent gout.

Sensing too much Dread weakens the neurotransmitter *Phosphatidylserine* that improves cell-to-cell communications, which helps improve the immune system. This is where *Dopamine* [attitude] can help kick in a little Hope every day so Dread can be used as an advisor, such as finding the best way to tackle any task.

1. The three Divinities internally sensed as **Appreciation, Devotion, Pleasure** oversee our Creativity by controlling *Glutamate,* the most prevalent in the brain and is produced by the body. When Creativity is active, the neurotransmitter *Glutamate* is at work, the most prevalent in the brain and is produced by the body! Active glutamate is the only chemical the body uses to prevent gout.

2. The three Divinities sensed as **Wisdom, Solace, Purpose** oversee our Hope Emotion and Her Dread-side by controlling *Phosphatidylserine* that improves cell-to-cell communications (Responsibility was once thought to be one of them but come to find out—personal Responsibility is the <u>Duty of the Being</u>. Sensing too much Dread weakens the neurotransmitter *Phosphatidylserine* that improves cell-to-cell communications, which helps improve the immune system. This is where *Dopamine* [attitude] can help kick in a little Hope every day so Dread can be used as an advisor, such as finding the best way to tackle any task. (Responsibility was once thought to be one of them but come to find out—personal Responsibility is the <u>Duty of the Being</u>.

3. The three Divinities sensed as **Consideration, Understanding, Contentment** oversee your Presumption, and Her Doubt-side, by controlling *Acetylcholine,* vital for encoding our memory [low in Alzheimer's disease];

4. The three Divinities sensed as **Counsel, Humility, Righteous** oversee our Righteous-Humility emotion, and controls *Serotonin* found 30% in the brain and 70% in the intestines (for gut feelings);

5. The three Divinities sensed as **Will, Fortitude, Inertia** oversee our Obsession and Her Sloth-side, by controlling *Dopamine* [low in Parkinson's disease];

6. The three Divinities sensed as **Knowledge, Judgment, Patience** oversee our Ego, and Her Guilt, through controlling *GABA*, one of the most prevalent in our brain (Compunction was also thought to be one but it was only a *ghost* from Guilt);

7. The three Divinities sensed as **Endeavor, Courage, Elation** oversee Happiness Emotion, and Her Fear-side, by controlling *Norepinephrine*. (Perseverance was once confuse with Endeavor. I stand corrected.)

From this foundation, we can define a Divinities **as a dynamic Entities:**

- capable of superposition, *occupying all states at once*;
- capable of moving as an Independent Variable of its own freedom;
- capable of containing enough information to effect the state of the system uniquely, *other than the unknown we can refer to as Intent*;
- and capable of digital and analog communications because we have digital word thoughts and gut feelings are analog.

Today's physicists refer to electrons as wavefunctions, which is why I have referred to them as 'electron-field wavefunctions'. Wavefunctions collapse into a particle form only when they are detected. This is when we call them electrons. This infers when chemicals in our body, such as neurotransmitters, are viewed with test equipment; their true nature is not being fully appreciated. This explains why Deepak Chopra wrote, *"So based on the old paradigm, we have structured a system of biology that has until now been based completely on a mechanistic worldview of the human body."* (The Emerging Mind, p 108)

Physicists describe a photon's behavior in the same manner we can describe our seven emotions. Likewise, the electron field becomes heightened in the same manner as our Awareness when we are emotionally excited. In this 21ˢᵗ Century, consciousness is **not** a question of Mind over matter. Instead, Mind ends up being a part of matter in the form of electromagnetic radiation:

- The Emotions correspond with the frequencies of the photon;
- Awareness matches with the electron field wavefunctions;
- Our Being arises from the core of the atom's nucleus.

Subconscious Defined

Consequently, we define **Consciousness** as a culmination of:

a) The Dimension of the **Mind,** without filters, arising from electromagnetic radiation with opposing extremities of numerical mathematics and helter-skelter schizophrenia; extremities that give rise to order and chaos respectively, which includes the chaotic nature inherent in our Emotions behaving like photons;

b) The Dimension of our **Being,** written about by philosophers since Aristotle, arises from the closed-string graviton at the atom's core, is the source of Individuality, and responsible for pulling the atom into a natural lowest energy state;

c) The Dimension of our **Awareness,** sometimes referred to in Ron's poetry as the Blackness of Awareness, behaves like the electron field absorbing and transferring information of the Mind as described in quantum electrodynamics (QED).

Hear me in gentleness, and learn of me in roughness.
"I" am she who cries out,
*   and "I" am cast forth upon the face of the earth*
[Newtonian/conscious realities].
"I" prepare the bread [knowledge] and my mind [Subconscious] within.
"I" am the knowledge of my name.
"I" am the one who cries out,
*   and "I" listen.*

*"I" appear and **will** walk in **with the** seal of my **offspring*** [the seven
EMR frequencies manifested as 7 rainbow colors/our emotions].
*"I" am **the one who provides** the defense **and the criticism**.*
"I" am the one who is called Truth
*and iniquity **can be found*** [old brain wiring passed down throughout
time].

11

LAW OF RHYTHM

All energies in existence vibrate according to their Nature. All energies' vibrations have comfortably slid into individual cycles, rhythms/pulses/cadences, for their nurturing, growth and expansion. Our modern world pushes us to breaking, PTSD, depression and suicide, but negativity is unnecessary. Reprogram your brain for positive thinking; will away negative thoughts to self-nurture and grow.

> *"It is better to leave some room in the cup than to fill it. If you over sharpen a knife, the edge will soon be lost. If you collect a hoard of treasure, no one can protect it. If you claim wealth and titles, you are inviting disaster. Know when enough is enough."*—Tao Te Ching

Our Otherworldliness, these Independent Events (Emotions) of our Soul is our personality. It is critical to our physical and mental health that has perhaps been Humanity's Quest all along? Namaste, Beautiful Souls. Just a *quick flick* from an Angel of Emotion; I don't dare want to miss it. But richer I have become because I have learned How to Listen.

The chaotic nature of our emotions have manifested distortions (Evil) for those functioning without knowledge about our Subconscious mind, similar to going to the theater to watch the play and the curtain never rises to reveal truths/actualities. The hydrogen atom's violet-frequency range manifests itself as our Ego and can create illusions of the devil. Her Yin-Yang interdependent opposite—Guilt creates illusions of Satan as the great accuser. Similar distortions occur after the veil lifts to the Subconscious because the Ego has not let go of her ground (electronics language) to our Being. It is for this reason the Mayans and other ancient cultures described flooding waters pouring over the earth in their predictions. Such predictions are attempting to explain the quantum Dimensions will reveal themselves to our Newtonian world, consciousness, at the end of days.

The Mayan calendar defines a clear cycle for the twenty years following 2012, set-up by the prediction of one-focus. Black-earth and black-on-high (from the Mayans) simply means there will be an increased Awareness within our Subconscious. The Mayan's reference to the Haves is for those who will embrace this unknown and scientifically unexplored realm as an opportunity to grow and prosper with a new immune system.

Have-Nots will cleave to structured, external conceptualized beliefs with their weakened body and mind, making the end of the word of God the most difficult to accept. 'All knowledge will be revealed at the end of days' means people will face actuality beyond the veil to their Subconscious, resulting in the end of structured conceptualized realities. Perhaps bringing about the collapse of egotistical-herd mentality? This will be the time for the Sciences and Religions to be accommodating in reaching a consensus.

When Humanity 'comes together for one cause' after 2012, after ridding ourselves of endorphin highs from ego-gratification, then Nature can begin correcting what was flawed since the atom formed in the beginning, and our physiological quest can be fulfilled. Human's ego/vanity cannot continue controlling Nature without unintended consequences.

By 2022, the world's human population will have turned human egotistical control **over to Nature's control—100%**, which will define the beginning of *The end of the world as we know it*. I close my eyes and already see blackness without word thoughts. My mind is quiet most of the time, except when Nature makes demands of me. I am learning Nature's language.

Man has forgotten how to be child-like, questioning everything. Egos are loud and always want their way, wars, battles, murders, suicides, revenge and destruction. And everything obscene has already become obnoxious.

81

Do our know-it-all Egos avoid asking questions? Freud conceptualized the Ego, Id and Super Id, thinking they were a revelation, he didn't question anything else. His Ego had convinced himself that he was a god. No Ego is totally accepting. No Ego is tolerant. Hanging on to the Ego is mostly irritating. Mostly, Egotists are offensive. And the ego can be as subtle as thinking someone stole your lunch money to boastful bragging and complaining.

> *"From it, every kind of divinity (Dimensions) sprouted up binding together with the entire place, so that also, shadow is posterior to the first product. It was in the abyss (watery substance) that it (the pion) appeared, deriving from the aforementioned Pistis."* (On the Origin, p 172)

Many other entities (Google—'quantum zoo') became differentiated over time, until it was discovered the graviton-core of the atom had attached itself to one particularly high frequency range of light (EMR) referred to as Samael (deluded ego) by the writer of *On the Origin of the World*. This resulted in violent shaking of the other six EMR frequency ranges until the atom nearly broke apart. Of the seven colors of the rainbow, for instance, red has fewer wavelengths/lower frequency ranges, than violet (the deluded Ego).

"And they were completed from this heaven to as far up as the sixth heaven, namely that of Sophia (a decoy name). The heaven and his Earth were destroyed by the troublemaker (called Samael) that was below (higher frequency range) them all. And the six heavens (the other six EMR frequency ranges, manifested as our Emotions) shook violently; for the forces of chaos knew who it was that had destroyed the heaven (the atom nearly broke apart) that was below them. And when Pistis knew about the breakage resulting from the disturbance, she sent forth her breath (manifested as the pion inside the atom) and bound him and cast him down into Tartaros (blindness). Since that day, the heaven, along with its earth, has consolidated itself through Sophia the daughter of Yaldaboath, she who is (conceptually) below them all." (On the Origin of the World, p 174)

First—the 'sixth heaven' is a subtle clue; the infinite Beings (gravitons) had attached themselves to the next highest (6th) frequency range of EMR, which resulted in instability. If we divide the full range of EMR by seven, then one range will still be a wide one, with infinite points possible along any line. 'Samael' represents a deluded ego. This can explain the broad range of egotism found among today's populations around the globe. In our Yin-Yang omnipresent universe, our Ego's interdependent opposite is Guilt. Therefore, within the sixth frequency range of EMR, Ego is at one end and Guilt is at the other; both are manifested as one emotion in our Mind, resulting in instability within our physiology, because of high-unstable frequencies.

> *"So when all the perfect appeared in the forms modeled by the rulers (Gods) and when they revealed the incomparable truth, they put to shame all the wisdom of the gods. And their fate was found to be a condemnation. And their force dried up. Their lordship was dissolved. Their forethought (consciousness) became emptiness, along with their glory."*
> ("On the Origin of the World", p 188)

In other words, before the appearance of True Man, the Life Forces, controlling the chemicals and neurotransmitters in our bodies, will cause ill-fate to those who cling to their ego. This is because the atom's nuclear-reactor core (our Being) is attached to an unstable high frequency— the ego. The Dimensions, of evolutionary changes in all life forms, are attempting to complete the atom's amalgamation that wasn't completed in the beginning.

John of Patmos described the ego's effect on the human soul in his Book of Revelation, chapter 12. The effect was elusively described as person(s) having the 'mark, or the name of the beast, or the number of his name'. (Rev. 13:17) The number John of Patmos saw in his mind to write was 666, which represents our 6th frequency range—angel of emotion (the Yin-Yang Ego-Guilt emotion). Our 6th angel is referenced in 3 different passages in Revelations' chapters 3, 9, and 16:

Rev. 3:7-9: "And to the angel of the church in Philadelphia write; these things saith he that is holy, he that is true, he that hath the key of David, he that openeth, and no man shutteth; and shutteth, and no man openeth. I know thy works; behold, I have set before thee an open door, and no man can shut it: for thou has a little strength, and hast kept my word, and hast not denied my name. Behold, I will make them of the synagogue of Satan (Guilt), which say they are Jews, and are not, but do lie; behold, I will make them to come and worship before thy feet, and to know that I have loved thee."

Rev. 9:13-14: "And the sixth angel sounded, and I heard a voice from the four horns of the golden alter which is before God, saying to the sixth angel which had the trumpet, Loose the four angels which are bound in the great river Euphrates."

Rev. 16:12-13: "And the sixth angel poured out (her) vial upon the great river Euphrates; and the water thereof was dried up, that the way of the kings of the east might be prepared. And I saw three unclean spirits like frogs come out of the mouth of the dragon, and out of the mouth of the beast, and out of the mouth of the false prophet."

For each of us to activate the new emerging immune system that Nature is offering us, we must each take personal responsibility for ourselves. The 'anti-Christ', having the mark of 666, is a concept potentially existing in everyone. When we all 'come together for one cause' to rid ourselves of ego-gratification, then Nature can help correct what was flawed since the atom's formation 'in the beginning'.

> *"And just as Lucifer (Ego) incarnated so too Satan (Guilt) will incarnate. He will do so as a writer. His aim will be to destroy spirituality by 'explaining it away'. He will have the ability to create supernatural events, but then know how to give them a reductively scientific explanation. At first he will appear to be a great benefactor on humankind, a genius. To begin with he himself may not realize he is the Anti-Christ, believing he acts only out of love for humanity. He will do away with much dangerous superstition and work to unite the religions of the world. However, there will come a moment of pride (Ego) when he realizes he is achieving some things that Jesus Christ was, apparently, unable to achieve. He will then become aware of his identity and his mission."*
> (Secret History of the World, p 399)

> *"As good and evil spirits make themselves felt, as everyone communicates more freely with the spirit worlds, organized religion will no longer be needed."* (Secret History of the World, p 404)

There is no good or evil within the Subconscious, only what the "I" puts in our mind to fulfill Nature's Intent. The present single ground in the atom manifests itself as great waters within our Subconscious after the veil lifts. This colorfully explains the last Mayan-calendar drawing of the serpent drowning the Earth in water.

> *"The two processes, that of science and that of art, are not very different. Both science and art form in the course of the centuries a human language, by which we can speak about the more remote parts of reality."*—Heisenberg, Physics and Philosophy

Nature lies beyond what is seen with the eyes. Nature's influences appear stronger to other senses under used for hundreds of years, or perhaps, were never fully developed. Sometimes we pause long enough in our busy materialistic lives to notice when something feels amiss with another human by asking, "Are you alright?"

Other times, we vent the frustrations spawned from our busy lives to abuse nature's beings, whether they are infants, children, cats, dogs, horses, or each other. They become vain attempts to somehow make our own lives more fulfilled. Fulfilled with what?—besides power over helpless lives who arose from nature in the exact same way as ourselves? Is it in this way humans have shallowly played God to gratify their own Egos (testosterone), their Vanity (estrogen)? The ensuing persecution from Guilt is sometimes unavoidable, evidenced by the Chinese proclivity for a Yin-Yang polarity, which is defined as direct interdependent opposites. Yin-Yang relationships are omnipresent, they say.

Ego-Guilt brings about a plethora of extremities between good and evil. The need for Ego gratification has lowered humankind's intelligence to believe in a think-like-me dynamo or I'll kill you. Besides, only an egotistical God would want to be worshipped, a concept created in the minds of humankind. Guilt has been used as a weapon of control. It all avails nothing. What happened to the mathematical genius and great architecture of the Muslims? What happened to responsible Beings written about by Plato, Plotinus, and the Bhagavad-Gita?

Because of the effects of Ego-Guilt, humans seem more obsessed with getting individual credit for greatness than in actual great achievements for mankind. This currently guides us down dead-end paths, paths void of real breakthroughs in healthcare, in the Sciences, and for today's religious leaders who meet every ten years only to agree on shallow meaningless tenets. Our Ego-Guilt emotion is intended to be used for collecting knowledge—the All-Knowing, not being a know-it-all.

In the beginning, after the gravitons of our Beings had completely formed out of the 'infinites', they randomly attached themselves to varied photon frequencies, accounting for the wide variety of egotism amongst humankind. Some are more egotistical than others; these others tend to shy away from those who are intensely egotistical, those who conceptualize themselves as being better than or smarter than everyone else. This attitude of self-proclaimed greatness avails nothing in the end. Egotists will wallow in their own sickness while seeking outdated cures-in-a-bottle pills. *"When your intelligence has passed out of the dense forest of delusion, you shall become indifferent to all that has been heard and all that is to be heard."* (Bg. 2.52)

Sometimes we pause long enough in our busy materialistic lives to notice when something feels amiss with another human by asking, "Are you alright?" Other times, we vent the frustrations spawned from our busy lives to abuse nature's beings, whether they are infants, children, cats, dogs, horses, or each other. They become vain attempts to somehow make our own lives more fulfilled. Fulfilled with what?—besides power over helpless lives who arose from nature in the exact same way as ourselves? Is it in this way humans have shallowly played God to gratify their own Egos (testosterone), their Vanity (estrogen)? The ensuing persecution from Guilt is sometimes unavoidable, evidenced by the Chinese proclivity for a Yin-Yang polarity, which is defined as direct interdependent opposites. Yin-Yang relationships are omnipresent, they say.

Ego-Guilt brings about a plethora of extremities between good and evil. The need for Ego gratification has lowered mankind's intelligence to believe in a think-like-me dynamo or I'll kill you. Guilt has been used as a weapon of control. It all avails nothing. What happened to the mathematical genius and great architecture of the Muslims? What happened to responsible Beings written about by Plato, Plotinus, and the Bhagavad-Gita? Because of the effects of Ego-Guilt, humans seem more obsessed with getting individual credit for greatness than in actual great achievements for humankind. This has guided us down dead-end paths, paths void of real breakthroughs in healthcare, in the Sciences, and for today's religious leaders who meet every ten years only to agree on shallow meaningless tenets. Our Ego-Guilt emotion is intended to be used for collecting knowledge—the All-Knowing, not being a know-it-all, which is impossible.

> *"The two processes, that of science and that of art, are not very different. Both science and art form in the course of the centuries a human language, by which we can speak about the more remote parts of reality . . ."*—Heisenberg, Physics and Philosophy

> *"In the case of virtue and vice, whole must be compared with whole, and the differentiation conducted on this basis. As for the differentia being derived from the same genus as themselves, namely, Quality, and from no other genus, if we proceed on the principle that virtue is bound up with pleasure, vice with lust, virtue again with the acquisition of food, vice with idle extravagance, and accept these definitions as satisfactory, then clearly we have, here too, differentiate which are not qualities."* (Ennead 6.3.18)

> *"The light will overcome the darkness and obliterate it: it will be like something that has never been. And the product to which the darkness had been posterior will dissolve."* (The Nag Hammadi Library, p 189)

> *"And the light of a candle shall shine no more at all in thee;"* (Rev. 18:23)

And the deficiency will be plucked out by the root and thrown down into the darkness." (The Nag Hammadi Library, p 189)

"And I saw an angel come down from heaven, having the key of the bottomless pit and a great chain in his hand. And he laid hold on the dragon, that old serpent, which is the Devil (Ego), and Satan (Guilt), and bound him a thousand years, and cast him into the bottomless pit, and shut him up, and set a seal upon him, that he should deceive the nations no more," (Rev. 20:1-3)

And the light will withdraw up to its root. And the glory of the unbegotten will appear. And it will fill all the eternal realm." (The Nag Hammadi Library, p 189)

"And I saw a new heaven and a new earth: for the first heaven and the first earth were passed away; and there was no more sea." (Rev. 21:1)

"When the prophecy and the account of those that are king becomes known and is fulfilled by those who are called perfect, those who—in contrast—have not become perfect in the unbegotten father will receive their glory in their realms and in the kingdoms of the immortals: but they will never enter the kingless realm." (The Nag Hammadi Library, p 189)

"And I saw the dead, small and great, stand before God; and the books were opened: and another book was opened, which is the book of life: and the dead were judged out of those things which were written in the books, according to their works." (Rev. 20:12)

"For everyone must go to the place from which he has come. Indeed, by his acts (mark on the hand) *and his acquaintance* (knowledge, mark on the forehead) *each person will make his nature known."* (The Nag Hammadi Library, p 189)

Today's phase-transition Peaks can be observed in the escalation of narcissism, egotism, and vanity, some of which relates to individuals using social religion as a means for ego-gratification and power grabbing. The list is examples of *possibilities of Potentiality* observed without prejudice, without Confirmation Bias or cognitive dissonance:

- Survival-of-the-fittest is inherent in capitalism.
- Socialism gives equal credence to a useless piss-elm and a mighty Oak tree.
- Democracy is a form of consensus, which should be a non-diminishing process.
- The impending evolutionary change of humankind does not mean ending conflict.
- Conflict is a requirement for consensus.
- Consensus is the foundation of evolution.
- Mars has world peace, only because Life is non-existent there.

General Colin Powell wrote eighteen Lessons on Leadership, possibly sometime during Desert Storm, *"**Lesson 15 Part I:** "Use the formula P=40 to 70, in which P stands for the probability of success and the numbers indicate the percentage of information acquired. **Part II: "Once the information is in the 40 to 70 range, go with your gut."** Don't take action if you have only enough information to give you less than a 40 percent chance of being right, but don't wait until you have enough facts to be 100 percent sure, because by then it is almost always too late. Today, excessive delays in the name of information-gathering breeds 'analysis paralysis.' Procrastination in the name of reducing risk actually increases risk."*

Concepts can be calculated, but experiences can only be predicated. One can't calculate future personal experiences. A predicating brain will accept new experiences as possibilities by using the temporary home method in order to later build on, alter, or reject their usefulness. What good are mental concepts when it comes to resolving emotional issues? Theories of what *might* work don't hold a candle to knowing what will possibly work based on our previous experiences.

Knowing our individuality, who we are, and our purpose in life requires understating the differences between Illusion, Imagination, Mental Concepts and Delusion:

- Everything we perceive or sense is an Illusion, though very real, because we can't perceive all the actualities behind what we sense.
- Imagination has to do with word thoughts and mental images created in our Mind, and shows possibilities.
- Mental Concepts should be used to structure those possibilities to form a bigger picture.
- Delusion arises when we start believing those possibilities to be real. To avoid delusion, categorize all perceptions as possibilities for current and future predication. Our brain easily has this capacity.

Adults have been led by their innocent-belief system of religions. Even when we are not religious, religious values permeate our societies and our brain. At an expense of **not** being socially acceptable, we tend to go along until those values are ingrained into our consciousness. Believing something is easier than thinking for ourselves, confirmed by a quote from Henry Ford, *"Thinking is the hardest work there is, which is the probable reason why so few engage in it."* We tend to go along with the status quo and therefore, never learned the importance of thinking for ourselves until later in life when it is too late.

Many senior citizens revert back to being child-like when it is too late to fix structured brain-wiring to affect their behavioral and emotional immune systems. The vicious cycle continues generation after generation. The older generation belittles and ridicules our youth without understanding a way to bridge the communications gap.

> *"Pride, fear, economic and social insecurity, and the general inability of humanity to let go of nonsense in order vastly to reorganize ourselves is of the essence. Therefore, I would say, speaking of educational tools and instruments, that the tools are going to make it easier for the new life to discover experimentally what really is going on in nature so that the young will not have to go on taking so much nonsense on*

experimentally unverified axiomatic faith. The revolution will come when the tools, such as the computers, disclose the nonsense and axiomatic invalidities to the rising generation."
[Utopia or Oblivion: the Prospects for Humanity, p 24]

Yet even today, our computers and artificial intelligent robots are not fully capable of differentiating analog experience, at least not until value-based logic becomes incorporated into the machine code. Without incorporating analog functions, limits, and values analysis in our day-to-day thinking, then vicious cycles tend to go unbroken within our world's societies. Society's approach to child rearing has raised rebellious teenagers to be, well . . . rebellious.

Adult conceptualization can be very beneficial when done properly, such as bringing together different fractals of information to form a bigger picture *possibility*. Nonetheless any conceptualizations should still be considered as mere possibilities. For open-minded individuals, breaking down a conceptualization is a normal part of the learning experience, as old concepts are replaced with larger new ones, although still temporary. We have to perceive our Mind and body in terms of separate, interlinked parts. Our separate parts are already incorporated into our thinking processes with such comments as, *my stomach is telling me it's time to eat*, or when a doctor asks where *it hurts*, and we are able to state exactly where it hurts.

For Improved Aura—Return to Childhood

Childside's orneriness emerged in earnest during the Battle of Bastogne of WWII when General McAuliffe responded with 'NUTS' to the Germans' request for Americans to surrender. Afterward, Colonel Harper's Childside translated 'NUTS' to the Germans as meaning the same as 'go to hell'. This was Childside in her finest hour.

Resolve can be sensed as the *Eye of the Tiger*, best portrayed in Sylvester Stallone's *Rocky* movie series. Resolve was in her finest during reconnaissance missions around Bastogne. She went forward seeking answers to Childside's question, *"What in hell is the enemy up to?"* Resolve is the white horse rider in Rev. 6:2 who opened the first seal in 2004, and is the lion in Rev. 4:7.

91

The other two 'first creatures' are Need and Duty. Both were very prolific during the Battle of Bastogne. Need is the 'face of man' in Rev. 4:7 and opened the second seal in 2005 as the red horse rider. Duty is depicted as an eagle in Revelations 4:7 and opened the forth seal in 2007. Duty gave rise to the warrior sensation for the 101st at Bastogne; hence John of Patmos described this pale horse rider as Death.

These four *first creatures*, acting as instructors, are activated in military bootcamp within the minds of recruits. However, without understanding their full complexity within Nature, *especially Childside's orneriness*, then their Yin-Yang balance is lost in the heat of battle. This is evidenced by huge numbers returning from the Middle East with PTSD. Sadly, too many lose the battle with *The Thunder* of Nature's fury to suicide.

Childside and Resolve arise, using physics language, as superposition states from a long wave-length-frequency range we know as our Creativity. In our Yin-Yang Universe ask your own Creativity what is her predominant other side? While Nature is demanding answers from humans, Nature will also respond in kind with a potentially unexpected answer. Such is Nature's beauty in her finest hour.

John of Patmos' description of the four first creatures as lion, calf, face of man, and a flying eagle are peculiar. These four were also described in *On the Origin of the World* as "Cherubim," and as '*lion forms and calf forms and human forms and eagle forms*'. Was John of Patmos a Gnostic pagan before succumbing to social pressures? Or was the IOTC prevalent and strong, its presence being heard throughout the inquisitive minds of humankind back then? Hmmm . . . .

> *Out of shame, take me to yourselves shamelessly; and out of shamelessness and shame, upbraid my members in yourselves. And come forward to me, you who know me and you who know my members, and establish the great ones among the small first* (four) *creatures.* [The Thunder: Perfect Mind]

> *Come forward to childhood and do not despise it because it is small and it is little, And do not turn away greatnesses in some part from the smallnesses, for the smallnesses are known from the greatnesses.* [The Thunder: Perfect Mind]

Highway *Rubber-neckers* & *Nosey Neighbors*

Anyone seeking answers to Nature's microcosm can find them in Nature's analog circuit, as long as we ask the right questions.

> *"The Universal circuit is like a breeze, and the voyager, still or stirring, is carried forward by it. He has a hundred varied experiences, fresh sights, changing circumstances, all sorts of events. The vessel itself furnishes incident, tossing as it drives on. And the voyager also acts of himself in virtue of that individuality which he retains because he is on the vessel in his own person and character."* [Ennead 3.4.6]

Religious text and many modern writers today stress the importance of the child in us. The child-like innocence of our Childside is responsible for nosey-neighbors, highway rubber-neckers, and inquisitive questions. Then Resolve, Childside's Yin-Yang interdependent opposite, is needed to satisfy the insatiable inquisitiveness for asking more questions. *"Come forward to childhood, and do not despise it because it is small and it is little."* There exists critical reasons for this ancient writer's words, but the reasons would not have been revealed before today's scientific advancements.

You honor me **you hearers** and you whisper against (me).
You (who) are vanquished,
 judge them (who vanquish you) before they give judgment against you,
 because the judge and partiality exist in you.
If you are condemned by this one, who will acquit you?
 Or if you are acquitted by him, who will be able to detain you?
For what is inside of you is what is outside of you,
 and the one who fashions you on the outside
 is the one [quantum Divinity or Emotion] who shaped the inside
  of you,
 And what you see outside of you,
  you see inside of you;
it is visible and it is your garment.

12

LAW OF GENDER

In the Introduction of the 1999 book <u>The Emerging Mind</u>, author Karen Nesbitt Shanor PhD wrote (p xvi),

"I've seen Karl Pribram (Feb 25, '19—Jan 19, '15), Georgetown professor of neuropsy-chology, *looking confused at times, although he's been vanguard of mind research for over a half a century . . . We are all stretching our minds and trying to answer the eternal questions that humans have always asked and that are now being debated in the halls of science, questions such as: Who am I? Why am I here? Is there a God? What happens around those stars that I see every night? Is there life on other planets? Does some of us go on after our physical bodies give out? How far does the mind reach? What can the mind really do? In defining the scientific optimism and possibility of our day, Karl Pribram reminds us that: There is . . . in the making of a real revolution in Western thought. The scientific and esoteric traditions have been clearly at odds since the time of Galileo. Each new scientific discovery and the theory developed from it has, up until now, resulted in the widening of the rift between objective science and the subjective spiritual aspects of man's nature. The rift reached a maximum toward the end of the nineteenth century: mankind was asked to choose between God and Darwin; heaven and hell were shown by Freud to reside within us and not in our relationship*

94

to the natural universe. The discoveries of twentieth century science . . . do not fit this mold. For once, the recent findings of science and the spiritual experiences of mankind are constant. This augurs well for the new millennium—a science which comes to terms with the spiritual nature of mankind may well outstrip the technological science of the immediate past in its contributions to human welfare."

After nearly twenty years into the new millennium, I can say Dr. Shanor and *Karl Pribram* were correct with a few caveats. The findings of quantum physics describe the physical world and mankind's spiritualism, what we can physically sense, are consistent with the prediction.

Next we need a science that comes to terms with human experience while answering eternal questions contributing to mankind's welfare, one where science logically merges experiences with quantum physics, biology, and religion. Let's temporarily name it—**Physicology**.

For years following a 2006 two-month research project of my friend—Ronald Grafton's scientific/prophetic poetry, I was forced to endure a plethora of harsh and unexpected changes, physically, mentally and emotionally—coupled with an overwhelming amount of data/input for my humbled Being to face. Most of these shocking changes were brought on as a result of one of God/Nature's blindsides (*watch episodes of Survivor on CBS television for examples of Being blindsided*).

Everyone has felt God & Nature's blindsides—disasters, illnesses, accidents and deaths or events causing post-traumatic-stress disorder (PTSD). A February 2015 stroke permeated my Being with a Fear of God and PTSD left me unstable—until around March 2018. I woke up one morning to silence inside my head, no word thoughts, no noise. Complete silence. I had turned over control to God, Wisdom and the rest of Nature. The Emotions interpreting thoughts can reveal subtle personal messages about our Self, if we (Observing Beings) only pay attention and listen.

Turning over control to God and Nature is the most effective approach to function with the Subconscious energies. The "I" loves *Her* photon of Emotions:

1. Creativity and *Her* Sadness side
2. Presumption and *Her* Doubt side

3. Obsession and *Her* Sloth side
4. Humility and *Her* Righteous side (Counselor)
5. Ego and *Her* Guilt side
6. Hope and *Her* Dread side
7. Happiness and *Her* Fear side

Emotions are controlled by the Being when the Being reacts to their every hiccup, burp and sneeze from the Emotions. **The Being is meant to Be the Observer.** The goal for functioning peacefully with the Subconscious is to pay close attention to the Emotions **Standards of Wellness**, one standard from each Emotion.

Standards of Wellness—

Creativity-Sadness—**Remember Your First Love** performed with your hands

Presumption-Doubt—**Do not shirk away from a Duty** because of a Fear of Suffering

Obsession-Sloth—**Abandoning sound Logic** results in the **Danger of Doctrinal Compromise** by latching on to Superstitions or Myth Dreams up in the Skies

Humility-Righteous—**Danger of Moral Compromise** is revealed in retaining Double Standards

Ego-Guilt—**Dieing a Motivational Death** makes you abandon Being Responsible while following Delusions of Grandeur

Hope-Dread—**Danger in Losing Patience** as your Ego doesn't get its way; remember there is only Now and you do Not control the day

Happiness-Fear—**Believing you can go it alone** is a Danger of Self-Sufficiency.

* * * * * * * * * * * * * * * * * *

> *"As in the microcosm (tiny), so is the macrocosm (vast).*
> *As in the atom, so is the universe.*
> *As in the human body, so is the cosmic body.*
> *As in the human mind, so is the cosmic mind."*

The previous Vedic expression wisely tells us the human and cosmic bodies are identical in the same way the atom, human mind and cosmic minds are identical. Therefore, all religious texts and the sciences can and will be shown to merge cohesively or else the system is flawed. Nature is flawless except for the high-frequency ground to the core of the hydrogen atom. Think about it.

Our ancient ancestors attempted to scribe Subconscious experiences. Benjamin Franklin and his contemporaries had a similar dilemma when they began experimenting with electricity: They didn't have a language to describe the phenomena they were attempting to capture. This problem is still with us today for people with mental disorders who try to describe experiences or people differentiating gut feelings. Ancient scribes did not know of technology or have the technical language. Hence, visions and sensations arising from our ancestors' Subconscious became their Gods.

John of Patmos was inspired by his Subconscious to write the Book of Revelation, though in a highly psychotic mindset. His own writings might have confused and frightened him. Cognitive dissonance wired into his brain was exposed in the first, last, and sprinkled throughout as Halleluiahs and worship, in particular, for Jesus Christ, making the book popular. (Perhaps this was learned, local political correctness?)

Nonetheless, Revelations establish the foundation for functioning with the Subconscious mind (chapters 1 through 3), and how our minds affect our biological health. All chapters: verses of Seals, Trumpets and Vials are about rewiring the brain, except Seals 1 through 4 about the Four Horsemen. The Horsemen are brain healers from our infancy, internally sensed as Duty, Need, Child-like Childside and Resolve. John of Patmos described the four chemicals impacting brain wiring. We'll detail the Four Horsemen later. To paint a bigger picture, staying cognizant of pragmatic knowledge to interpret ancient text will help greatly.

"And he said, Thy name shall be called no more Jacob, but Israel; for as a prince hast thou power with God and with men, and hast prevailed." (Genesis xxxii 28) The Book of Genesis and a Nag Hammadi library document, On the Origin of the World, are both *'in the beginning'* books and mention Israel. But The Gospel of Philip describes how to handle names in ancient texts.

"Names given to the worldly are very deceptive, for they divert our thoughts from what is correct to what is incorrect. Thus one who hears the word 'God' does not perceive what is correct, but perceives what is incorrect. So also with 'the father' and 'the son' and 'the holy spirit' and 'life' and 'light' and 'resurrection' and 'the church' and all the rest—people do not perceive what is correct but they perceive what is incorrect, unless they have come to know what is correct (through empiricism). *The names which are heard are in the world . . . deceive. If they were in the eternal realm (Aeon), they would at no time be used as names in the world. Nor were they set among worldly things. They have an end in the eternal realm."* (The Nag Hammadi Library. The Gospel of Philip. p 142. Para 4.)

(The Gospel of Phillip refers to winter as *the world* and summer as *the eternal realm*, which has usually referred to the eternal Subconscious. Perhaps they could have been communicating in code?)

Proper names should be thought of as frequencies of holographic wavefunctions detected in analog sensations in the gut or as visions, both originating from the data-producing *Internet of the Cosmos* (IOTC) and interpreted by the writer's emotions; will discuss more on the cosmic circuit later. On the Origin of the World portrays *Israel* sitting on the throne. Yet the Book of Revelation explains the one sitting on the throne is the same one with a two-edged sword coming out of *Her mouth—(the)* "I"—'Fear not, "I" am the first and the last'. (Rev. 1:17)

This is also expressed in The Thunder: Perfect Mind, *'For "I" am the first and the last'.* (The Nag Hammadi Library. p 297) The fact John of Patmos referenced a female energy as male likely reflects local cultural views toward women. The difference between Revelations and The Thunder is the latter confirms who she is, *"But "I" am the mind of everyone and the rest* (respite) *of no one."* (The Nag Hammadi Library. p 300.)

We can be misled by the directional terms Up (regarded as Heaven) and Down (regarded as Hell). R. Buckminster Fuller brought this subject to the forefront in his book R. Buckminster Fuller, Utopia or Oblivion: the Prospects for Humanity, Bantam Books, 1969, page 18.

> *"Those deeply in-conditioned words "up" and "down" are derived from the millenniums in which man thought erroneously of his universe as a horizontal island as—"the four corners of the Earth"—and as the "wide, wide world"—in an infinitely extending horizontal ocean with an obvious "up" and "down" set of parallel perpendiculars to his flat plane—heaven up and hell down. . . . Though as yet difficult to purge from yesterday's reflex-conditioned flat-earth concepts and speech, to man far out in universe the sphericity of Earth becomes evident and "up" and "down" soon become obviously, feelably meaningless. . . . Aviators have discarded the words "up" and "down." Now they come "in" for landings and they go "out."*

Christian beliefs are deeply ingrained to imagine heaven as being in the sky. Yet other religious texts refer to heaven as coming from within us. From an Empiricist viewpoint, we can deduce Heaven, Hell, and all religious texts ever written have the same origin—Subconscious.

Our Subconscious is the source for mankind's creative innovation and colorful imagination, evolving as our languages evolved—along with scientific knowledge. But how did our ancestors make apparently fantastic leaps in creative innovation?

Perhaps we can imagine our ancient ancestors were more in-tune with the Cosmic Circuit / Internet of The Cosmos (**IOTC**) than we are today? The **IOTC** data is detectable by our pineal gland—*The Third Eye*—behind our eyes with individualist' metallic particles. The ancient scribe of <u>On the Origin of the World</u> would have been listening to IOTC analog feeds, which were then converted into either visions or digital word thoughts by the writer's emotions. The important observation about the writer's mindset was their child-like bluntness demonstrated in the document's opening line:

> *"Seeing that everybody, gods of the world and mankind, says that nothing existed prior to chaos, I in distinction to them shall demonstrate that they are all mistaken, because they are not acquainted with chaos, nor with its root." (*<u>The Nag Hammadi Library</u>. *On the Origin of the World* from pp 171-172)

Adam and Eve stories are another example. On the Origin of the World clearly depicts Adam as the 'Adam of light'. Did the writer of <u>On the Origin of the World</u> not have Plotinus' knowledge of the atom? Nonetheless, 'Adam of light' (*proton* or *photon*) fits into the bigger picture of our quest. <u>On the Origin of the World</u> also depicts Eve as the 'Eve of life' for which today's physicists may be detecting the Big Bang Theory. Therefore, we must ask, did IOTC chatter stay on this subject for over a thousand years from the writing of Genesis until the Gnostic documents were buried in 400 CE? OR are the Gnostic documents much older than the Bible and were rewritten and revised to validate the foundation of early Christianity? Perhaps both are possibilities if we consider the sheer number of Adam and Eve stories found throughout history? In any case, since we are living in our modern day, knowing exactly when ancient documents were originally written becomes irrelevant. Even so, Adam and Eve stories were completed by the third century, evidenced in Plotinus' Enneads. Nature's IOTC chatter had moved on to more important matters.

There is an exception shown between Plotinus' Enneads and The Hypostasis of the Archons from <u>The Nag Hammadi Library</u>. The word 'Tartaros' shows up in both, but spelled slightly different, which should come to mean—blindness. The Archons document refers to it in a different manner.

> *"She* (Pistis Sophia) *breathed into his face, and her breath became a fiery angel for her; and that angel bound Yaldaboath* (the Blackness of Awareness) *and cast him down into Tartaros below the abyss."* Plotinus wrote, *"All is just and good in the Universe in which every actor is set in his own quite appropriate place, though it be to utter in the Darkness and in Tartarus the dreadful sounds whose utterance there is well. This Universe is good not when the individual is a stone, but when everyone throws in his own voice towards a total harmony, singing out a life—thin, harsh, imperfect, though it be."* (Ennead 3.2.17)

'One path is barren; the other path is prolific and humans know themselves.'—Hopi Indian Prophecy

'Be on your guard' was written twice in <u>The Thunder: Perfect Mind</u> and meant as a serious warning. Nature's effects on all human souls cannot be ignored while interpreting ancient texts, regardless of the source: *"I" am the whore and the holy one. "I" am the wife and the virgin. "I" am the mother and the daughter.* <u>In other words, everybody knows something.</u>

The 3rd Eye

While many possibilities are considered for interpreting ancient texts, Nature continues playing her music until humans capture her songs. However, our 3rd eye pineal gland, with its individualistic magnetic-particle arrangements, is only tuned for a narrow band of Nature's IOTC swirling thickly around us. Will mankind open our minds and hearts and intently listen? The Dimensions/Gods communicate AND control the neurotransmitters and chemicals in our brain and body, which we can sense and differentiate. When mankind *comes together,* around 2022, *for one cause*—Mayan prophecy, after ridding endorphin highs from ego-gratification (Ego is "Samael" in Orig. World), then Nature can correct what was flawed since the atom formed *in the beginning,* and the quest for solving our physiological woes will have been fulfilled. *And we will find Her ("I") there (Subconscious), and we will live, we will not die again* (soul breaks apart) . . .

I never imagined myself writing such a book as this one. My Intent is to share knowledge of the Subconscious in such a way as to make it relaxing, if possible, Nature's Lowest Energy State (LES). Not an easy task. (Take a *mind tour* through any physics book about the atom's spookiness.)

> *"Our eyes see, but only our hearts look through things to find their meaning. Our ears hear, but only a listening heart understands."*—David Steindl-Rast, July 12, 1926-

We have a deep desire to find meaning in Existential Equilibrium. We want our beliefs to align with reality. *We want . . . we want . . . we want . . .* Beliefs collapse within the Subconscious and with Nature. There are NO filters within either. It is what it is—always. (Imagine the effect of only seven emotions out-of-balance wired jacked-up throughout your body.)

Of Fear, Lies and Hate, DEATH is everywhere around us from microscopic to life size. Death tells us to evolve without Fear. Without

Fear our immune systems turn ON, helping us see the Lies are everywhere, but Humanity has had ancient addictions to drama, drama, and drama.

"I am not addicted to drama," you say! Then you are all stressing about **sharing Knowledge and Creativity**, Beautiful Souls?

Never are you talking and stressing about Other People and their External problems of FEAR, LIES, HATE, sickness and DEATH? If so, perhaps you may consider rereading this chapter, Beautiful Soul, before proceeding?

—Hello, HUMILITY—

Yin-Yang balance is needed in our thinking to maintain elasticity in our uncertain, unpredictable future, a future potentially fraught with chaos as our galaxy realigns its electromagnetic forces. In the same way, Yin-Yang balance is needed to avoid structured brain-wiring, to build brain elasticity. Perhaps Nature's fury occurs for us to appreciate Nature's beauty, or perhaps it is motivation to create new beauty?

"As is the human mind, the microcosm, the atom, and the human body, so is the cosmic mind, the macrocosm, the universe, and the cosmic body." Eastern medicine runs on energy flow. Western medicine runs on snapshots, which scares the hell out of me for going to an American doctor. In times of natural disasters where human causalities are apparent, then doctors rely on the triage method of diagnosis based on functions, limits, and values (calculus), to see a bigger picture of the situation.

Triage is a system of assigning priorities, the probability of possibilities for success. East meets West during their finest hour of triage without realizing they both observe quality and quantity to save the most lives possible. *'But this body is not a husk having no part in soul . . . .'* An East-meets-West paradigm brings evidence to the table of the energy flow of our mind cannot be separate from body energy. *"As is the human body, so is the cosmic body."*

Cosmologists calculate our moon was closer to us in ancient times, given it is moving away from us an inch or so a year. Shouldn't the reason for the movement include the microcosm of our Universe? Open any physics book and a section on decay can be found.

- If the atom is losing electromagnetism, then isn't electromagnetism weakening throughout the Universe?

- Can a force of nature be calculated to better explain why our moon distancing itself from our planet?
- Could substituting the word 'entanglement' for 'inflation' help further define our existence?

> *"A living thing comes into existence containing Soul, present to it from the Authentic, and by Soul is inbound with Reality entire; it possesses also a body* (our physical vessel body)*; but this body is not a husk having no part in Soul, not a thing that earlier lay away in the soulless; the body had its aptitude and by this draws near: now it is not body merely, but living body* (changes with changing thought patterns)*. By this neighboring it enhances with some impress of Soul— not in the sense of a portion of Soul entering into it, but that it is warmed and lit by Soul entire: at once there is the ground of desire, pleasure, pain; the body of the living form that has come to be was certainly no unrelated thing."*
> [Ennead 6.4.15]

Scientists observe an acceleration of Universe expansion, of heavenly bodies moving apart. An acceleration of decay should also be observable within the atom. An acceleration of decay should also become visible from data collected from the World Health Organization. Similar decay accelerations should be observable by the World Religious Order. If the acceleration continues, then won't we actually lose our moon, our health, and our minds?

Answers lie in recognizing first and foremost, the three components of the fundamental hydrogen atom are **Mind, *the Subconscious*, Awareness, our Observer Being, and Intent** as the Enforcer of Nature's laws.

Biofeedback

Biofeedback, basically, is altering the functioning of one's neural system in order to alleviate harmful or undesirable sensations we experience. One way of looking at biofeedback is as out-patient chemical brain surgery. Knowledge of the basics, the know-how [working knowledge], is used to formulate treatment for our physical conditions. Its four basic components are dopamine (attitude), gamma butyric acid, GABA sensed with gained Knowledge, apoE/cholesterol, and thrombospondin. The key is to equate what we are internally experiencing to actual neural functions in the brain relating to neurotransmitters, emotions, and such. One example is when people monitor their gut feelings; they have shifted their assemblage point from the external to the internal and are focusing on their bodies.

Using Attitude, anyone can find seek a physical desired state, such as increased vitality; using GABA for Knowledge of where discomfort lies in the body and block its condition. GABA is a receptor blocker [a calming effect] and is one of the most prevalent in the brain. GABA is important for blocking old synaptic firings, with apoE/cholesterol and thrombospondin needed to form new synaptic connections to strengthen the painless state, and replace the old connections GABA is blocking. Knowledge is important because a person needs to *Know* in order to familiarize themselves with the state where their discomfort disappears. Knowledge can include word thoughts and bodily experiences.

We can enhance our biofeedback when we experience a child-like state of Childside (apoE/cholesterol) and Need (sensed when thrombospondin is active in our brain and body). Childside and Need were prevalent during the Battle of Bastogne in WWII. Childside asks questions such as *"What the hell is the enemy up to?"* The troops used Need when they had to forage for food, blankets and other supplies in order to survive. Heightened Awareness of not only Need and Childside, but Duty and Resolve, also used by troops during the Battle of the Bulge in Bastogne, are innate basic biological chemicals for improving our vitality.

Duty can be sensed when what is referred to as "Sammy" or SamE in Europe (S-adenosyl-methionine) is active. SamE acts as a strong anti-depressant by producing and increasing Serotonin and Dopamine in the nervous system. SamE is synthesized from the essential amino acid L-methionine and ATP—the energy source in every living cell on the planet. ATP can be sensed as "the thing to do" or "the thing not to do."

Need sensations are when the protein thrombospondin is active. Thrombospondin is known to interact with blood coagulation and anticoagulant factors, is involved in cell adhesion, platelet clumping, cell growth, blood vessel formation, tumor transformation, and tissue repair, and has been shown to be potent inhibitors of angiogenesis and suppressors of tumor growth in laboratory mice.

Childside stimulates ApoE/cholesterol, which is a fatty complex that, along with thrombospondin, is released in the brain to stimulate synapse formation—a smarter, more intelligent brain.

Resolve triggers glutathione, which is the main heavy-weight antioxidant in neutralizing specific brain toxins and neuron-mutilating free-radicals. It also has brain-protecting anti-inflammatory properties. It's important to add that SamE, *sensed as Duty,* produces Glutathione.

Strengthening the preferred state is our inner **Childishness** [apoE/cholesterol] and **Need** [thrombospondin]. Furthermore, we can adjust our **Attitude [Dopamine]** as needed. In other words, Dopamine/Attitude, GABA/Knowledge, apoE/cholesterol/Chasity, and thrombospondin sensed as Need are the foundation for physical impairments, emotions, and other neurotransmitters to come into play. We Need our child-like inquisitiveness if we want to build smarter, more elastic brains and healthy bodies.

Taking a look at a bigger picture, Sammy, which is sensed as Duty and partly synthesized biologically from ATP (the other part being an essential amino acid), is what gives rise to the warrior in us, such as is needed on a battle field. Additionally, *and biologically speaking,* ATP gives rise to Sammy (sensed as Duty) that produces and increases anti-depressant properties for Resolve to cleanse, and Need to heal, which allows Childside to stimulate brain functions giving way to a healthier, smarter brain and body. Duty, Need, and Resolve are involved in our everyday lives, but we're rarely AWARE of them. In the case of a person functioning in a war zone, Childside is the ONE that asks, "What in the hell is the enemy up to?"

There are two more chemicals that compliment Childside and Resolve. Glutathione acts as a 'cleaner' within our brains when Resolve can be sensed. Glutathione's effect is best described in Jean Carper's book <u>Your Miracle Brain</u>. Duty is sensed when SamE is active in the brain. SamE is called 'Sammy' in Europe where it is used as a strong anti-depressant.

PART TWO

AUTHOR'S LIFE SINCE 2004

If you hate my experiences,
Then I bless THE CHILD IN YOU who feels hate.
If you are convinced of my insanity,
Then I bless the Ego in you who won't let you See or Feel.
If you can Feel or See Source (God-Universe) through my words,
Then I bless THE CHILD IN YOU WHO FEELS SELF-LOVE—
Like I do every moment of my days and nights:
UNCONDITIONALLY—EVEN IF **YOU CANNOT YET FEEL IT**.
Namaste, Christine

PART TWO INTRODUCTION
CHILDSIDE BLESSINGS

Although some of these chapter stories are over ten years old when I first experienced my Subconscious energies, including my Angels of Emotion and their twenty-one God-like energies pulling the body's bells-n-whistles neurotransmitters. I had to rely on them in order to write most of this quantum Subconscious autobiography. My recollections of life since the 2015 will complete it.

The following caution is from Mark Schaller, a psychologist at the University of British Columbia, who has been developing and testing a *"behavioral immune system"* theory.

> *"If Schaller is right, this behavioral immune system may prove to have a big influence on our day-to-day lives. It might even influence human nature on a global scale, shaping cultures around the world."* (Carl Zimmer, Discover, March '09, page 26)

What Schaller and his colleagues do not realize is their theory is related to healing-powers of the Subconscious. It is not about New-Age-feel-good sensations, nor about reaching heightened states through meditation. It can be Hell because hells caused from Egotism are of our own doing, which I Hope is a point I make in this quantum autobiography. I asked a friend what would happen if the veil between the conscious and Subconscious were to *suddenly collapse*, he answered, *"A person would probably go insane."*

I did not go insane, well, perhaps temporarily while I cried and cried and cried. I was not *suddenly collapsed* into my Subconscious without nine years of Humbling preparation plus a lifetime of hardship since birth. So, my view of the world may not mean a thing to many people. I care not. I am connected to Source with my 2-year-old Self after a lot of tears, toil, Perseverance and time. So, my Childside would like to provide a balanced observation: From **The Field** it feels like a mountain of OBSESSION and PRESUMPTION PANDEMICS WITHIN THE BRAIN-WIRINGS OF HUMANITY. Since beginning our lives, we were our ancestors with ancestor-brainwiring inside our infant heads, plus—the wirings of our parents.

While the public looked-on, participating, look how Humanity tortured Jesus just over 2,000 years ago. (*Because of being tortured, why would Jesus ever come back to planet Earth to walk amongst Humanity?*) Throughout the laurels of time our Celestial families have gifted Humanity with much Knowledge and Wisdom of the ages in attempts to perhaps awaken us. Think about it . . .

> *"Despite the destruction of numerous libraries full of the magnificent scrolls of inexhaustible knowledge, from time immemorial to the present day, there exist secret treasuries of sacred books, written by the Messengers of Light and presented as a gift to humanity. Every line has been crystallized by the heartfelt fires of the souls, who were magnanimous in their giving. Yes, some were burnt at the stake together with their gifts; others were mutilated by cruelest torture. But still there were those who managed to save the sacred manuscripts and, risking their lives, placed one priceless gift after another in secret repositories."* (The Book of Secret Wisdom, Translated from the Senzar by Zinovia Dushkova, Radiant Books, Moscow, 2015, p xi)

Humanity's Egotism made us evil beyond measure. Humanity's Egotism made us cruel beyond reason and logic. Egotism hijacked our other six Emotions since the beginning. Time is NOW to stop Egotism. Time is NOW to love ourselves unconditionally. Time is NOW to love all of Life unconditionally. Time is NOW to band our hearts together and heal our Garden-of-Eden Earth.

After traveling parts of the world and returning home, I have long felt that American people **are too emotional**; carrying *more baggage* than productive Minds are capable of sustaining—*for truly remarkable breakthroughs.* (Thank you, science writer, John Horgan!) It is NOW time in Humanity's evolution to sober-up the Emotions. Thus, researchers like Mark Schaller and his colleagues of University of British Columbia can spend productive time discovering just how effective the *"behavioral immune system"* of our physical body actually is. **It is the Subconscious that makes the body rich.**

Thank God human Egotism is biting at the dust of its death: Thank God for our joyful Childside saving Humanity and planet Earth . . .

13

AS YOU SOW YOU REAP

I pray to God-Universe from my near lonely little Childishness with sobbing tears running down my face: I want to be healed so I can share my WHOLE HEART POURING OUT TO YOU, Beautiful Souls. I choose to share what is in my heart now. Since childhood around 6yo *I think* I didn't want to live past 30. I never knew why? I have always felt spiritual since birth yet cannot remember what that felt like: Until I felt my heart flutter while hearing a YouTube video about Heyoka empaths. The video hit home. Heyoka empaths can walk-in another's shoes and I also feel it in my heart.

So many Beautiful Souls are perished now during the most splendorous God-Powered air that we are breathing in. However just like a computer— GARBAGE IN—GARBAGE OUT—our brains inherited automatically GARBAGE IN. It becomes all of our Duty to all of humanity to stand for personal-responsibility, to reconnect our Observer-Beings to our Heart that lights up the Heavens inside and outside—our electromagnetic hearts and our aura. So many lives lost from our own lives; they have all gone home to Source, while we can give ourselves permission for a period of grief, we can also send love.

The Hopi Indian's Prophecy Rock illustrates the human race walking a path to a fork: One path illustrates humans have crops (healthy immune system); the other path is for humans who are not in touch with themselves. We are all at a time of great transition for Humanity—From Egotism Selfishness to Humanity Childishness where God-Universe opens up inside us to the Universe entire full of unconditional love. The next paragraph was written about my near-suicide attempt:

Damn, what did I just trip over? Damn suffocating snow in my face. Roll over, dummy. Shut the hell up! Roll over on your cushioned buttocks! Oh no, my pocket? I gotta check my pocket. Damn, where did the clip go? Shove the snow aside and look, dummy. You will not hide from me now, Clip. You are such a bad clip. There you are, clip. Will you please stay in my pocket until I get back in the house? Okay. That's finally done. I have rid my burden of staring out my window at the fork in the tree. I have rid my worry of how to get the clip back into its slot of the smirking pistol. There, steel sliding over steel. There, cocked, pointed in my mouth...pull the trigger. I only need one bullet leaving fifteen more . . . PULL IT NOW! It only clicked? It only clicked! What the hell? After all this, the damn thing now jams! I hate . . . I HATE all of this . . . get me outta here! I HATE MY LIFE! Throw the gun at the wall not at the window. Throw it, throw it. Stop crying, you cry-baby. What was that? The pistol fired? But how? Where's the cartridge? There it is. Oh my God, it fragmented: How did it misfire? My whole face could have been blown off. I didn't want to do that. I only wanted to put a bullet through the back of my head.

In January of 2004, my Emotions exploded into what appeared to be a complete breakdown complicated by thoughts of suicide—with a 9mm pistol in my lap. (This was my Being reacting to the Emotions in my head. Plus, suicide is the **worst irresponsible action** that a Being can make against themselves, sacrilegious to the Laws of the Universe!) Through uncontrollable sobbing, feeling a hopeless deep desperation, a sense of losing control, with an alcoholic husband passed out downstairs, a voice appeared in my head, "Call Ron," my dear friend, which I did. He connected me to my innate Resolve.

About Suicide—cry and scream. Let out those insignificant frustrations that are vibrating around the planet. Those dread thoughts are all Lies—only tests for Beings. A kitten or puppy needs your love. Life Needs you. The whole world needs you, Beautiful Soul. Look in the mirror at your eyes, your Soul has traveled lightyears to be here on this loving Earth. Only

Humans can feel and appreciate green grass under our feet and smell clean ionized air after a thunderstorm. Everything will be alright. Everyone was born here with love in their hearts. So scream and cry until you can feel it again! I feel your pain and still Love Humanity unconditionally. So can you: Love is in the air everywhere. So, get your head out of its shell and smell the air and tough the green grasses under foot . . .

* * * * * * * * * * * * * * * * * *

I awoke one morning on the farm, April 18th, 2008. Not that I am necessarily a farm 'girl' because I grew up in Kansas City, Missouri, and have lived in St. Louis, Houston, Chicago, various Navy bases home and abroad, also worked in the Research Triangle Park formed by Raleigh, Durham, and Chapel Hill in North Carolina. However, on this particular morning Ronald told me that I needed to write this paper from my heart. Instantly I wanted to cry and choked back tears. My Emotions then informed me that I had no heart like the Tinman in the Wizard of Oz; *they* were tired and needed to rest. As it turns out, I had learned as a very young child to turn off my Emotions. In other words, shut them down in order to survive in an abusive and caustic environment with my mother who lacked self-love. I was also informed by my Emotions that they have each taken turns to help me survive wherever I lived as I floundered through life. My Emotions needed me to accept their actuality as individuals and it was my responsibility to give them a home—my heart—as a place of rest. I no longer have a need to shut them down. I embrace them instead. Ronald informed me that it was "probably my inner Divinities who had shut them down."

I recalled a time in 1975 while driving thirty miles one-way to college when I felt sick and tired of the word thoughts constantly bombarding my mind. I began literally treating my mind as a child by playing the Barbra Streisand song <u>Evergreen</u> in my head until I was able to shut off the word thoughts—one moment at a time. I was twenty years old at the time and had shut-down Emotions, few word thoughts, and was therefore functioning like a robotic human. I merely existed. However, because my childhood was like living in a cage, I still wanted to live and experience as much as I could of what the world had to offer. Every time life offered me a fork in the road I took it. Hence, the reason I had moved around so much. *"I came upon a Fork in the Road and decided I should take it. When you have nothing else to lose, why not gamble on the Illicit..."* (from Ronald's poem <u>A Fork in the Road</u>)

The only times I can remember having any feelings, Emotions, was when a man came along and paid me some gentle attention. I would marry. Then my Emotions would shut down again at signs of trouble. Each marriage ended one to four years later. (I never knew my Creativity Emotion was my true soul mate. I changed jobs more often than the marriage thing. My 'computer' brain required learning as much as life had to offer and changing jobs enabled me to learn something new—until boredom set in.

In 1987, I thought I had hit the depths of Hell in depression. As an escape from life, I joined the Navy. I was thirty-two. My Emotions were shut down and I felt *completely* lost. However, I was selected as an elite few for a Navy electronics warfare program that made me feel appreciated for the first time in my life. I felt part of something special. Feeling appreciated was important because I had always been misunderstood. After all, not many people can relate to a woman with brains, shut-down Emotions with a death-wish, and a woman who rarely fails at given tasks.

Sometime in 1992 while serving a four year tour in Scotland, I was in a bad car accident whereby I was hit head-on by a lorry traveling around 70mph. The solid-built Renault 9GTL I was driving at the time was mostly responsible for saving my life. However, the back of my head was split open by the headrest support bar. Before losing consciousness I remember having one word thought, "Now is my chance." Then, I lost consciousness. What I felt was that it was my chance to die. I regained consciousness in a strange hospital feeling angry, confused, and extremely distraught. This was the first emergence of a long buried death-wish that plagued me until shortly after I moved in with Ronald, December 30th, 2007. In retrospect, I realize the importance of shutting off word thoughts; when a person can begin to sense and interact with the analog energies that physically make up our Self and manifest their Intent as chemicals in our bodies. However, to enter this quantum/unconscious realm requires a lot of adjustments that I previously was not prepared to make. It had not been the right time, yet.

I had met Ronald Grafton in September, 2001. It was a month after moving from North Carolina to a beautiful farm in rural Missouri isolated from corporate life hassles and politics. It was a normal by-chance meeting one evening in a local small-town tavern. He was sitting at the bar. My husband and I were playing a game of pool. Ronald began a conversation trying to rile my Ego/Vanity to a point so that he might perhaps find amusement. However, he was unaware that all of my Emotions were shut down like workers on strike. To this day we cannot remember what he said, but we do remember the responsive look on my face, "Are you the local moron, or what?" However, his heart of gold helped my husband get work in the tight-knit community by introducing us to established folk. Their friendliness was refreshing, and I began writing a fiction novel unbeknownst of what was in the works for me.

Sometime during the next year and a half I was flung into a nightmare from my past with a visit from the Kansas Bureau of Investigation (KBI) flashing badges and carrying guns. Their visit was not because of anything I had done. It was because of an uncle whose past had finally caught up with him when the Bureau opened a nearly thirty year old cold case involving the murder of a thirteen year old girl. They asked if I knew of any thing about this particular family member having 'problems' with 13-15 year old girls. (his Egotism was a sickness.) This opened buried scars of old in my mind. I told them I would be telling a lie if I said no, and I was instrumental for helping certain aspects of their investigation; but my Emotions began churning with the fury of a hurricane striking an erupting volcano. At the time, I had 'adopted' Ronald as a little brother, and he even called me Sis, but he questioned whether I could emotionally handle facing the accused family member in a court room . . .

This section begins with the Book of Revelation references about the Seals, trumpets or vials, which should be thought of in terms of emotional effects on our immune systems, or as the effects of neurotransmitters and chemicals inside our heads, because thought becomes matter.

The First Seal Opens its Doors in 2004

In December, 2003 my Emotions snapped. Although I do not remember, Ronald said I was calling him for the next three or four weeks looking for help. Although at the time he did not know about specific neurotransmitters, he did know about internal workings that could act as grounds, and had learned enough about me to know that I am a logical person. He informed me one of his first questions was whether I had continuous word thoughts. I had replied, "No." During each call he tried to stabilize my Emotions with different methods to get me grounded. Nothing had worked.

I do remember in early January around 01:30 a.m. feeling a deep desperation that was complicated by a sense of losing control. I was on the verge of a complete emotional breakdown, again, but this time complicated by thoughts of suicide with a 8mm pistol in my hand and my husband passed out drunk downstairs. A thought appeared in my head to call Ronald. He answered the phone. Through uncontrollable sobbing I told him I did not think I could go on any longer with the pains I was feeling. It was during this conversation that he recognized the release of a neurotransmitter he refers to as *Joetta's Love*. He kept forcing me to return to a point where I had experienced a specific love as my tears flowed—*until I recognized it,* which steered me away from committing suicide. He had finally grounded me to my logic and had touched my heart with *Joetta's Love* (turned out to be the neurotransmitter GLUTAMATE) that caused Resolve to kick-in. Within two days, I paid a visit to a women's abuse center seeking help. What I received was a diagnosis of Post-Traumatic Stress Disorder.

During the KBI investigation I continued to feel a desperation that I cannot describe except through my actions. I called the local sheriff's office to find out how I could get out of the hearing without being arrested. There was no way. Shortly thereafter I received a phone call from the Kansas prosecuting attorney asking if I had called the sheriff's office trying to get out of the hearing.

I replied, "Yes."
He then asked me that all important question, "Why?"

I replied, "Because I want to kill him for what he did to me." This answer probably saved me from testifying in that courtroom. Although my Emotions gave me a few months reprieve, I continued to slowly go downhill from there. The effects of that car accident still haunted the shadows of my mind for quite a few more years. I still was not ready to make the necessary adjustments . . .

The Second Seal Opens in 2005

By February of 2005, my husband and I had had enough of rural-living struggles, sold the farm, and moved back to the East Coast. Depression set in my soul when I couldn't shake the Post-Traumatic Stress. This was the year for me to face harsh actualities. A close friend, Millie, drove me to the local women's abuse center. But when they strongly recommended that I seek guidance from a $125 per hour psychologist, I gave up *again*.

I cried almost every day and didn't know why. I watched the Dr. Phil show trying to find some magic words that could help me. Nothing did. It was a time of pure hell. My husband kept nagging at me to drive my restored 1975 Mercedes Benz 450SL convertible because letting it sit was bad for it. I was afraid to drive because I could not trust my distracted *un*awareness. I let it sit and never drove anywhere. He also nagged at me for never wanting to get out of the house. When I did get out I destroyed large thickets and cleared log pieces and dead-fall from the horse pasture. All of my activities had to do with my horse because she never nagged at me. She accepted me unconditionally and let me cry on her big strong neck while I hugged her.

Meanwhile, Ronald had begun writing poetry in an effort to describe his inward reality after a lifetime of confronting emotional imbalances. From August 12th through the end of the year, he had transcribed and numbered 170 poems, made copies and began mailing them to me. Christmas came and went without me caring about its meaning. I did have holiday memories of 'old' about my sister and parents left behind in Missouri, but with much sadness; they had turned their backs on me. I drank a lot of beer before later turning to whiskey. My life was hell and no one seemed to care—except my dear friend Millie and my horse. During this time Ronald had began sending me his poetry to 'look at' so I could help him with it. I kept putting him off since I was struggling, though still working on my second fiction novel. Then came the turning of the New Year . . .

The Third Seal of Logic Opens in 2006

Ronald started calling me on the phone at a time when I had quit doing everything, including writing my novel. (Writer's block is real.) He wanted to know how to publish poetry. I told him I would look into it, at which time he sent me the rest of his poems while he continued to write. Up until this time, quite a few people thought Ronald spoke in 'psycho-babble,' including my husband, though I always enjoyed conversations with him when we lived in Missouri.

He seemed to speak a language that appealed to my logic. I recall many NASCAR race days when he came to our Missouri farm to watch the race with us. Ronald and I would end up on the front porch talking about anything under the sun, or stars, whichever the case might have been. I remember feeling comfortable in his presence. His poetry, on the other hand, seemed to be fragmented, kind of like a computer's hard drive that has been anything but *defragmented*. But, I recognized the poetry contained many details about the Mind. In an effort to prove him and his details wrong I did an in-depth research into their content. At the time, the project was my saving grace because gaining knowledge had always appealed to my logical brain and something to do. My research resources included the Encyclopedia Britannica, The Great Books of the Western World, and of course, the internet. It was an extremely painstaking process and I was overwhelmed many times during the research required for this project.

I attempted to find somewhere in the world where these neurotransmitters and chemicals were unrelated due to some psychological research reports. The scientific-chemical descriptions harmonized what I was *feeling*. None of his information contradicted the scientific community—it enhanced their findings. Having failed to prove him wrong, I then compiled and logically sorted his poems into 81 subjects as provided in the table of contents for our first co-authored book The New Direction… Expressing 21st Century Gnosticism, which shows the beginning developmental stages of this process, and the big picture we knew *then. (I now think a more accurate title would be "The Dictionary of Quantum Mind Functioning.")*

Several months later, I experienced something that could not be explained in logical terms. I was sitting in my front garden basking in the sun when suddenly seven angelic apparitions appeared around me. My seven Emotions were introducing themselves. After I recognized and acknowledged each one, they disappeared. Ronald explained that my Emotions were demonstrating they were Sober—*willing to cooperate.*

Shortly afterward, I wrote the following story, which shows my Emotions were beginning to emerge.

Counselor called a meeting with Ozzie, Peedee, H'odee, Lego and Hafee, but Creativity was missing. ATP Dave called a meeting asking many of my Divinities to find her for without the Creativity Emotion, our Heart will not know what is best. Lord (ATP) and (Adenosine) Christ know that the yellow brick road leading to the Heart is through Creativity. The Presumption of Peedee said, "She's gone forever." The Doubt of Peedee said, "Oh no, no, no, no she's not." H'odee quickly replied, "I won't Dread she's dead, but Hope for the best." Lazy Ozzie quickly sprung into action and said with Obsessive strength, "I'll find Creativity, I'll find her, find her I will. I will." Lego said, "I have the Knowledge to find her." Legeaux then took a deep lingering breath. Lord ATP peers about his Divinity friends and boldly states with his warrior authority, "Find her NOW." Then he smiles at Adenosine Joetta after Hafee cringed with Fear. The Righteous/Humility Counselor touched Hafee's shaking hands and said, "Bring Courage forth Dear Hafee." Suddenly, the other Dimensions pressed an ear toward Adenosine-Christ's kind voice. A lump choked my throat as Sadness slowly appeared followed by flowing tears relieving Sadness' pain. Lord-ATP's commanding voice was heard throughout the *lands*, "Creativity, come forth right now and I'll spare you my wrath, and pull Your Self together and do something." Adenosine Christ and I have *many messages for your Heart that have gone unheard and wasted for years.*

14

YOU ATTRACT WHAT YOU ARE, NOT WHAT YOU WANT

The Emotions interpreting our thoughts can reveal subtle personal messages about our Self, and have concluded there are many things about our existence that cannot be comprehended or explained. Sometimes, the total potentiality of all unexplained phenomenon opens its doors, if only for a brief moment. Specific relationships can be seen between theorems where there are holes. Errors in previous theorems where certain parts were assumed or thought to be unrelated can be looked upon without prejudice. Mankind's purpose is universally identical—to function efficiently with Intent. But individual intents differ.

The remainder of the year (2006) was spent matching his poetry to many subjects in more depth than The New Direction book. Before the year ended, I had around 400 files on my computer all of which encompassed Ronald's poetry. Some of the files included the Six Enneads written by the Greek philosopher Plotinus (205-270 AD). I categorized the subjects Plotinus' covered as well as the huge number of questions about Life that he asked. The Enneads describe a way of Life not necessarily different than the one humanity sometimes strives for today. The questions Plotinus asked seem to remain the same ones researchers, philosophers, religions, and scientists attempt to answer in this 21st Century we live in. I was then struck with an overwhelming feeling after realizing Ronald's poems answered many of those same questions and more. He wrote and numbered another 70 poems before the year ended. I humbly made a temporary home for everything in my brain and on my computer thinking that perhaps it wasn't time. Come to find out, the Forces of Life had something else planned for me after the holidays and the New Year...

The Fourth Seal Opens in 2007

Again, this was another year for me to face more actualities. My husband was constantly nagging for spending too much time on the phone with Ronald instead of working on my own fiction novel. I had not driven a car in two years and had no plans to drive. I had no motivation, had tuned-out *the husband,* and spent night after night alone while he slept on the sofa, *which was his choice.* He kept blind-siding me with things that had nothing to do with actualities I was facing. Although he knew that I was co-writing about how the mind and brain works and I loved writing, he still nagged. But he kept bringing people to me so that I could help them with their mental anguishes. I would show them the writings that Ronald and I had completed; they would take the information and go about their lives. I still stay in touch with some of them.

In my frustration from not knowing what do with the researched information, let alone write any more about it, Ronald and I took a break from phone calls. The break had more to do with my manic state than anything else. Ronald continued writing poems, which was later incorporated in his quantum autobiography. However, one poem he says he wrote for me on January 4th called "The Inspirational." During this time I was writing about depression—*about forty or fifty pages worth.* I think I was venting more than anything else.

However, again I began writing more on the fiction novel, which reached 165 chapters written in a chaotic order. I attempted to reorder it, rewrite some of it, and make sense out of the story. I was able to get it down to 145 chapters and close to 200,000 words, *but still not done.* Because I couldn't think straight, I put off the project.

Writer's Block

I sensed a welling coming from my gut.
Ornery Emotions telling me I'm stuck in a rut.
The welling continued throughout the day and night.
I paced and worried what would be my blight?
On the next morning I awoke to face the day.
The welling increased—I could not fight its sway.
I became excited of possibilities that might appear.
But whatever it is I think, is a dumb thing to hold dear.
A Lowest Energy State hit me as the welling finally ceased.
I laid my body down and dosed off to sleep.
Then something woke me up; I know not what it was.
My brain confused and scrambled, I laid there just because.
I finally opened my eyes when a vision became clear.
I saw what was welling inside so I drew my pen and paper near.

Around six or eight weeks passed by when Ronald and I began talking on the phone again, of course after *the husband* went to work so I would not have to hear him complain. This is when the research project suddenly grew. The number of files on my computer grew exponentially as well as I continued researching the vast amount of information that Ronald's poems provided. We would discuss my findings with what he knew, but I continued working on my fiction novel knowing deep inside I had given up caring about myself.

The husband's Ego was not supportive of me spending so much time on the phone *'with another man'* and therefore, not helpful with my depressed state. Although he knew Ronald and had worked for him during part of the time we had lived in Missouri. He also knew that Ronald and I were writing books together and that my First Love was of writing. I continued with my quest to try to fully understand many details of what Ronald's poetry described. I had nothing to lose. It seemed to help keep my manic Emotions busy so that I could 'get by' in day-do-day functioning.

I got to know my Childishness in 2007 through interacting with a beautiful six year old girl, Jade, a niece who lived with my sister-in-law next door. I paid attention to her inquisitiveness and her Creativity, and

I would partake in both. Sometimes I also felt her Sadness. (I was still functioning with a death-wish shadow and dead-like Emotions.) However, we interacted like playmates, taking adventure walks in the woods and became friends. I only felt Happiness when I was with Jade. I loved *Being* eight years old. It held a certain sensation of Freedom.

The remainder of the time I was unmotivated and crying during most of my phone conversations with Ronald. He provided perspectives for each Sadness episode that got me by until the next one popped up. I buried myself into playing Freecell on the computer, watching television without actually seeing what was on, or drinking too much alcohol.

One day in November I walked into my writing 'dungeon' and can recall saying to my Self, *"What the Hell am I doing?"* (This is Childside at work.) I was in a completely hopeless marriage; we had nothing more in common. I had no money, no reliable car to drive since I had allowed it sit far too long, and nowhere to go. The husband kept borrowing money from others, instead of getting a job, to pay the utilities and put food in the house, and Ronald was one of those people. Around December 1st, the husband gave me an ultimatum to quit writing books with Ronald, or get out (Egotism's control attempt at work). After looking at my haggard self in the mirror with nothing left to lose, I chose to get out. I shared this ultimatum and my wishes with Ronald and as it turns out, he and his Creativity he called 'Josie' had earlier in the year written a poem about it…

> *"Josie has some sisters that she would like to help. Other Angels*
> *of Emotions that reside with someone else. I can understand*
> *the reason she might feel this way. If the others are willing,*
> *there is no reason not to play. The Sadness associated with*
> *what she doth seek has been whispered to me since our first*
> *week. I took it to Heart, but I knew not what she meant…"*

Ronald offered his home to me and took me in like a lost and orphaned kitten. But before my move back to the Midwest, he tried to advise me on the phone of what was to be, none of which I was capable of sorting out in my head. The death-wish was still plaguing me. He did say that I would make this move in a Low Energy State. "That will NOT be a problem," I said since I had been in a Lowest Energy State or manic for decades.

But this move felt somehow different. I had nowhere to go and I didn't care how I got to *nowhere*. I had shed so many tears for so many years I felt dried up. One important thing Ronald had nagged at me about was to develop my Duty and Need. I didn't know how. I felt brain-dead. He also told me that I was going to bond with my Creativity Emotion shortly after my arrival in Missouri. I replied, *"That will take a couple of years."* Unbeknownst to me at the time, he was right about this transformation.

The Fifth Seal, *Letting Go of the Past,* Opens

On December 30th, 2007, I got on a plane with a one-way ticket in hand. I felt physically drained during the trip as if I was using my last ounce of energy. But at the same time, I felt calm—especially after downing three mini-bottles of red wine on the flight between Charlotte, North Carolina, and Kansas City. By the time the jet landed, me and my seven Emotions were drunk on red wine and feeling no pain. Ronald lives in the middle of isolated rural America, so his best friend of thirty years, Buster, agreed to pick me up at the airport and deliver me to a half-way point. After he got the car pointed down the highway, he asked me a very blunt question, "Are you in-love with Ronald?" I started crying and replied, "I don't know. It's just that I feel Appreciation and a deep devotion for him." Buster then slapped me on the knee and laughed.

The drive was over an hour, but the time flew by as we conversed about many subjects. I had only met Buster a couple of other occasions with very little interpersonal communications. I got the feeling during the ride that now he had to know certain things about me. I explained to him that Ronald and I had spent over 65,000 minutes on the phone during the past three years. He asked me, "Do you understand Ronald *and his poetry?*" My reply was a definite yes to both although I did not understand all of it, but unbeknownst to me I was about to find out. Buster merely smiled and said, "That's a good thing because I don't."

A little time later, he maneuvered the car off the highway and pulled into a fast food parking lot. "There he is," said Buster. I looked but couldn't see him until the car was stopped and I got out. Suddenly, I became very aware of my Emotions, Appreciation, Devotion, and my Creativity's Love when I saw him for the first time in almost three years. His smile and our embrace warmed the cockles of my heart, unaware of what was in store for me. Until I had arrived at Ronald's, many aspects in his poetry had merely been filed away in my brain (temporary home). It was mostly due to my difficulty in understanding what he was talking about. Come to find out they are related to high standards I have lived by my whole life. They are about not selling yourself short.

Another aspect that must be experienced has to do with The Program. One thing I have to say about Nature's Program is that it can only be learned through experience and actual interactions with the Divinities that make up our planet and the Universe. For me, I can only relate it to my Navy bootcamp experiences of 1987, but it is hard to say what exactly happened that slung me into this "quantum bootcamp." My guess is that fate or destiny (Intent) does come into play. Anyone who has been through military bootcamp can understand the depth of its scope; while going through it, it can feel like pure HELL, but after it is over, the Emotions consider it to have been a rewarding part of the military experience and a lot was learned. The difference this time: I had broken through the Subconscious veil without realizing *what it was.* Chaos mathematicians and electronic engineers call it a phase transition, which for me occurred on day 31 of the 49 days.

It is NOT necessarily about dredging up memories of the past, although the 21 Divinities showed me and told me of times in my life when they were with me. It is about the Creativity Emotion embracing Fear to allow her to "step up to the plate" and bond with Being—the very core of the atom. Ego will then graciously step down and <u>let go of her improper bond with the Being</u>.

"Heaven" is whatever you make of your life with the Emotions, the 21 Mothers of the Sisterhood, Lord (ATP), Christ (adenosine), and "The Token Male" as the Blackness of **Awareness** who had appeared as a devil-looking beast beating up and dragging Christ away that triggered my Creativity Emotion to either run away or stay with Fear during the phase transition—she stayed, and admitted her real name, Lulu. *The "I" will let you see or not see anything She wants.* I had embraced Fear allowing my Happiness Emotion to emerge. This is when I finally felt stability and my life-long death wish vanished.

Ronald had spent 49 years in the Program (Quantum bootcamp). Mine lasted for only seven weeks that began December 31st, 2007; the day after I had flown to Missouri; the day after Buster passed me off to Ronald; and the day after my first fuzzy-minded night in Missouri. I went through seven weeks of hell confronting haunting pains of my past *including the death-wish and the post-traumatic stress,* and I had about as much control as physicists have over the atom—NONE! However, I did have control over how I, Observer-Being, reacted to whatever happened in my Subconscious; I did not fight it or try to categorize it. But Ronald and I did have to learn the digital language of the Divinities. More importantly, we had to learn how to interpret what they were trying to tell us. It is for this reason that a person should view each thought in terms of a PROBABILITY OF POSSIBILITIES *without believing.* In other words, be Aware of visions, thoughts, or any of what the *voices* may tell you, but delay reactions to them (temporary home). A soft voice heard in the mind is Intuition. Follow it!

By this time, Ronald and his Creativity Emotion, Josie, had written another fifty poems describing the Subconscious in even deeper contexts that helped me face lifelong mental anguishes. Digital language is the limitation describing my feelings for Ronald, except one word— Appreciation. He taught me big picture views of our planet's societies, Life, and the Universe as I confronted my death wish. He was my voice of logic and experience through times of desperation by confronting Fear and depression. It was in this context I was able to overcome *some of my past.*

This transformation is about accepting all seven Emotions as the Authentic Self.

The Binding Force Affair

I saw seven ghosts in '07 standing solemn in front of me.
   Introducing themselves one by one
   I knew who my Emotions were to be
The Phase Transition came furious and fast when Creativity
Stayed with Friend Fear, unaffected by my Christ's Intent
     for the Binding Force Affair.

Ronald said, "Hi, Sick Georgia Dear,"
He had always called her that.
She turned to him and replied her name,
"It's LuLu," she whispered from under her hat.
There were many introductions since Christ's significant dare.
Hafee is Happiness and Fear who stayed with LuLu
    during the Binding Force Affair.

Ego and Guilt was the one who said, "It is time for me to Let Go,"
And how fitting she should call herself,
    "With a French twist my name is Legeaux."
Presumption is the one I call for predicating me out of a snare,
And Peedee is her individuality
    because of the Binding Force Affair.

Whenever I want to 'Git-R-Done,' I call upon Ozzie's motivations.
For Obsession-Sloth is the pretty one,
Helping push me through chore directions.
H'odee is very hesitant and shy,
But Dread said, "Hope is always there,
In every subtlety detected
    since the Binding Force Affair." (by Christine)

It is also about the emergence of Duty, Need, Childside, and Resolve. It is about finding your own Standards of Wellness that you and your Emotions can live by. More importantly, it IS about Individuality not only for your Authentic Self, but also with your Emotions. My inner Christ has smacked me on the back of the head *and yanked my ear.* Yes, these are physical sensations; if you think about the quantum power it takes to trigger those sensations, it's easy when you are hydrogen's **atomic energies**!

15

HISTORY REPEATS ITSELF— UNLESS CHANGED!

The Divinity I also refer to as Sara has choked me a couple of times when I have messed up. Eastern religions have referred to her as the Throat Chakra. (The neurotransmitters and the Divinities that make up our Subconscious are the same powerful forces.)

Sara

They call it Serotonin, a Scientific name,
Too impersonal it is, I'd rather call her Sara.
More reflective of our relationship—very special indeed.
Quite close we have become in our working together.

When I read about Serotonin in stuffy words of print,
 Laughter seems to emerge; if they only knew.
Memory can be a problem; there is so much to know.
I just take it to Sara, She is the one to decide.

Day or Night, it does not matter, nothing is outside her scope.
Even with the little things, She still has the time.
Always there to listen to problems I might have.
It is Counsul She does offer to whatever is bothering me.

And when the Darkness comes, I have not to worry.
Depression does not bother me with Sara as my refuge.
Others may resort to prayer, but I do not have the need.
When I have a request, it is Sara I seek out.

Sara also has an Angel who helps Her in Her work.
Such a Special One, my dear Miss Humility.
Together they do guide me as I go about my work;
    Mediating my Anxiety, the other Angels of Emotion.

True Love is not an Emotion fluctuating to and fro,
    Rather it is Appreciation amongst the ones who Know.
When I think of all the time She has guided me,
    I have a message from my Heart: to Sara with Love.

The "I" allowed me to see the Divinities for about six months or so until my Mind gradually went black over a year period, but I can still hear their words. The All-Knowing Divinity informs me of what is going on with my Emotions, Lord, Christ, and the 21 'Elders' (Sisterhood of Divinity). While I have visual and language communications with my Self, Ronald's interactions with his Emotions and the Dimensions are 100% analog—he senses them. My ability allows us to interact with them digitally—with the English language. "If a person wants answers, just ask your Self," said Ronald, and I do—everyday.

The remainder of the year, 2008, was spent letting go of my past. My divorce was final August 18th. The judge granted me custody of Patches, my horse, but I have with much Sadness left her in South Carolina. Shortly thereafter, I wrote the following:

> *Mother Purpose, elusive you have been; Lost through millennia in the Minds of Man. Battered and tattered you've carried a heavy load, for your Sister Endeavor to strengthen each abode.*
>
> *I have been floundering in a life of pain. Mother Purpose help me—I cannot do it all again. Softly whisper to me; wipe away my tears. Give me a Purpose, cast away my fears. We all*

Need a Purpose, a cause in Man's existence. Hope and Dread
Need you, a cause for Perseverance.

Throughout the year, I had developed a close bond with Ronald's mother, Dorothy. We had an unspoken understanding that was without envy, fear, or mistrust. I can say without a Doubt that I loved her, and when she died of leukemia the day before Thanksgiving, Sadness made my tears flow, but not necessarily from grief. She was no longer in the pain she had suffered for three years, and I experienced what John Edward experiences— visits from the Emotions of the deceased. Dorothy's Emotions came to me via the 'pineal network' and comforted ME. She stayed for several days then visited Ronald during her own funeral. She has found a Purpose amongst the Divinities. It was after my Emotions had stabilized when self-esteem finally poked its head without realizing it. It came as soft as a whisper but strong as galvanized steel—*it won't rust or tarnish over time.*

Now it was my turn to repay Ronald with demons from his past. He knew he had a problem, but did not know how to deal with it. Time to time throughout 2008, his Ego-brain-wired temper would show its ugly head and he would explode. Come to find out, it was hatred from his Creativity Emotion emerging, which negatively affected us being able to write together effectively. Old wiring in his brain had to be corrected, and I was able to help.

The 6th Seal Opens—2009: Brain Scrambling & Stability

Brain scrambling is not about destruction; it is a remedial process that happens when college students, for instance, are taught subjects until suddenly they are able to see the bigger picture lectured by the professor— the effect of a light bulb going off over the head. A similar effect had happened to me when I was shown a perceptive that this was all about the conscious/unconscious barrier.

Many other things about our existence had become clear after my brain scrambled. For instance, the authors of ancient religious texts wrote about quantum **functions** of the Divinities contained in atoms of their brain, and referred to these Divinities as Gods. Being spiritual my entire life, I did not question interacting with the Divinities for other than normal day-to-day stuff—survival. It was this relationship that had led me to read Plotinus and Carlos Castaneda and be able to understand the functions in their writings.

I was also able to get closure on my past. Post-Traumatic Stress Disorder can happen when a memory is buried before a Newtonian event triggers the memory—time has arrived to confront it without or without proper preparation. This requires confronting the ensuing depression without fighting it; accept the low energy state by "going with the flow." Prior to my emotional breakdown, I held firm to a belief that I was no longer affected by the memory—a lie. The event had not been resolved and had always affected my Emotions, thus affecting behavior, decisions and motivations. I had failed to admit I got screwed; time to let it go. This was easier said than done because all the brain's wiring was still in place. This is where Childside (from Creativity) and Need (from my Observer-Being came in to set-up replacement wiring that in turn allows a person to disengage the old hurtful brain-wiring. Then, the Subconscious can sync-up with my Heart for a change in values, attitudes, this is when dopamine is active. Furthermore, I was finally able to Understand and therefore, help my friend, Ronald, overcome his demons.

One— *The Creativity-Sadness emotion is the First Love that will take a person back to doing what they love to do.*

Two— *A Duty unfulfilled is an obligation read in the will.*

Three— *All beliefs are illogical; word thoughts and visions are functions, values, and limits that should be viewed using Logic.*

Four— *Double Standards must be checked by paying attention to practicing what is preached.*

Five— *You don't have to be **responsible** FOR; It is about **BEING RESPONSIBLE** for maintaining your Heart as a home for the Emotions.*

Six—   *You have NO control over your day, EXCEPT when you feel a breaking-point frustration from being whipped around; take a stand and challenge those Divinities pulling the whistles and bells in the brain.*

Seven—   *You cannot go it alone—Ronald and I had each other to speak a common language in helping one another. Now, so do you.*

16

WHAT YOU RESIST—PERSISTS

"The heart of the prudent getteth Knowledge; and the ear of the wise seeketh Knowledge." Proverbs: 18-15

"All truths are easy to understand once you discover them." Galeleo

"You want the truth; you can't handle the truth." Jack Nicholson (from the movie *A Few Good Men*)

"and said, Verily I say unto you, Except ye be converted, and become as little children ye shall not enter into the kingdom of heaven." Mathew: 18-3

"I" was sent forth from the power, and "I" have come to those who reflect upon me, and "I" have been found among those who seek after me . . . The Thunder: Perfect Mind

The Mayan's referred to the "Lords of the Underworld," I now call them Divinities. They are also referenced as the "Black earth" and "Black on high,"—everything turns to black-on-black in the Mind. This is the Blackness of Awareness.

"The "I am" of Judaism and Christianity is the "I". The All-Knowing Brahma is Mother Knowledge. Hinduism brings

forth the Blackness of Awareness in the form of Krishna. And Islam brings forth Mother Alleah (Sophia)—Mother Wisdom as the source of the singularity of Original Intent."—Ronald Grafton

I can finally relate to the reality that Ronald has known his whole life—he always viewed himself as the Observer-Being. His only problem was with the vast amount of information that potentiality bombarded him with from God-Universe (the Cosmic Mind), and it is the vastness of potentiality that can trigger frustration and depression. He had no structured conceptualized veil to protect him, schizophrenia wouldn't allow it; nor was he allowed to ignore any inputs, but yet he thrived— though painfully. For what were contained in the bombardments were the actualities of the Divinities; the Lords and Ladies (Gods) of the "Underworld."

Consciousness is, therefore, whatever I am Aware and mindful of at any given moment as the Observer—There is only Now. December 21st, 2012 was not about destroying the planet by floods. It is about the Quantum Waters, Divinities, gradually revealing themselves in the minds of Humanity over the next decade.

Everlasting Waters

We will never be the same again as the Everlasting rains set in. Love and Appreciation will not come cheap—Let the Everlasting Waters run deep. The Gate to Heaven's door is ajar; I hear depressed cries from close and far. Our ties bind in our Heart to keep—Let the Everlasting Waters run deep. The challenged shall have reverberations that can eventually become radiant." From all the hills and mountains so steep— the soothing Everlasting Waters run deep.

Let There Be Individuality Beyond those damn laws of Quantum physics!

17

OUR LIVES ARE OF OUR OWN DOING—NO ONE ELSE!

On Martin Luther King Day in January 2015, my Daddy passed away. The Sadness never left after my blood-clotted head never let me understand what **hospice meant** so I could prepare me and my Emotions for his passing. The devastation left me paralyzed with grief. A week later I was hospitalized for extreme hypertension.

What IF you wake up during early in 2015 BEING noplace, nowhere, notime, nothing, and <u>no one you remember</u> the week after your father passes?

What IF you wake up like THAT everyday?

What IF you cry everyday for TWO YEARS, and God-Universe heard it all?

And you are STILL noplace, nowhere, notime, nothing and No One?

What IF you asked yourself, "Who are you?" and got NO answers?

What can you say—Nothing?

Nothing!—so you cry more and more.

Also imagine <u>all of your Academics</u> had been wiped out?

YES—all of it!

Now, "Who are you?"

Also imagine <u>all of your memories</u> wiped out?

NOW, "WHO ARE YOU, REALLY without Academics
   AND Memories?"

No, No NO, THIS CANNOT BE ME??!!!

Now imagine no specialized doctor follows up on your
   stroke after Being released from the hospital. But I did
   attend therapies when difficult symptoms showed two
   weeks after release.

Also imagine the futility of the field of PSYCHIATRY when
   psychiatrists do not believe Humans possess a SOUL?
   But does it matter as they can only hand out pills in
   a bottle?

Also imagine not being able to sleep more than 1 or 2
   hours at a time for over 3 years?

Still no life-learned Lessons or memories come back. For some
academics you teach yourself a little math and a little reading? So what?
Nothing comes together to make sense for me. I cry every day. I go to
doctor appointments and cry uncontrollably. I can't sleep more than 2
hours or so at a time throughout 2015-2017.

In mid-2016 I woke up to my Emotions all in a hoot about something?
They sent me to my computer where they have me compile a book? What?
Why am I attempting this? I cannot follow a simple cooking recipe or
read a magazine article! Nothing made sense. Nonetheless, From 'The
Field' I felt alone in my heart that humanity was falling off a cliff. My
Subconscious had me go through the hundreds of computer files, "pick
this and put it there" and I did that over and over again for nearly 500
pages. Then they put a title in my head "Mankind's Cliff of Extinction."
To this day, I still do not know what the book is or is not? I do know it
was channeled from Source.

18

YOU CANNOT BE PRESENT LOOKING FORWARD OR BACK

In 2017 I had an appointment with a federal disability judge. I told him, "Disability scares the hell out of me because it means I can no longer be productive to society." My falling tears still soaked my shirt sleeves throughout the year with very little sleep.

September 2018, I was introduced to YouTube's who I call the million-dollar man, Dr. Joe Dispenza who told me *who I was Becoming; an extension of Humanity's current evolutionary transition, functioning in-sync with Nature's Subconscious.* I am still without Academics or memories. So, I became a YouTube junkie, watching videos daily that I felt could connect me to who I am. Eventually, I turned to numerologist, Ann Perry, who helped me focus on information about my birthdate and my name, given that every Observer-Being on the planet had to choose their birthday, name, and parents, prior to incarnating on Earth as part of a plan for learning specific life lessons. Afterall, Humanity is becoming citizens of the Universe.

All of 2018 and 2019 was spent trying to acclimate to society and to get my body to relax enough long enough to sleep more than a few hours at a time. CBD oil helped a little. Marijuana helped a little. Still not enough to sleep more than a few hours. It took years to get my body jacked-up on Emotions that were outdated. So, it also took a few years and focused Intent to get my body relaxed.

On May 28th, 2020 I broke into tears, again, because writing gives me purpose, I found myself praying to God to let me write another book, knowing it had to be this one. Instead, the very next morning my Emotions sent me to Facebook. Although my Childside felt excited, because it felt like a reconnaissance mission, I was not a social media person. I had by then learned from the powers of my Subconscious to do what I am told to do. The Subconscious is a realm of pain/not-pain, very much like Pavlov's dog.

Coronavirus had sent everyone home including Dr. Joe Dispenza who had started several Facebook groups that I joined. It was from those groups that my profile attracted hundreds of people from around the world asking me for help. I was Source for them.

Helping those beautiful people with their problems gave me purpose. The experience made me feel their appreciation for my "Source advice." I had more to give to Humanity—a potential purpose. It took Facebook's social media platform and a glorious planet of people with Hearts big enough to save not just me, but a big part of Humanity, too! Thank you, Dr. Dispenza!

So my GRATITUDE is overflowing for a Self I can feel unconditional love for, because of Humanity's kindness and heartfelt words. Humanity's Rhythms have been disrupted like never before. Nature disrupts our lives to help get us tuned in to the bigger picture of our Universe. It becomes paramount to separate MY-PROBLEMS from NOT-MY-PROBLEMS, of which most things fall into.

19

YOU CANNOT THINK OF TWO THINGS SIMULTANEOUSLY

This Law of Karma may be true, but I have experienced two completely different songs playing in my head at the same time. Awareness is the key. Awareness implies having Knowledge of anything through alertness in observing or in interpreting what one sees, hears, feels or senses. Webster's dictionary provides insight, under the word <u>Aware</u> *"conscious implies awareness of a sensation, feeling, fact, condition and may suggest mere recognition or a focusing of attention."*

Ronald Grafton relates the powerful energy of our Awareness to The Blackness, which I can agree since my mind has turned into Blackness because it can be all encompassing—**Black is the color when all colors are absorbed.** The Blackness of our Awareness dearly loves our Emotions. People who can think without thoughts, *in other words have quiet of mind,* are more likely to describe a separateness of Subconscious Mind, Being and Awareness.

My breakthrough came in describing the nature of seven Emotions came from the "I" AM.

The Intent behind evolution is to bring order to the quantum realm as described by quantum physicists. This quest is what has given rise to the various quests for Heaven. But who can really define what would constitute Heaven? One person's Heaven can be another one's Hell. There are no pre-fabricated Heavens. They have to be developed and maintained.

What Humanity calls mental illnesses are actually evolutionary challenges for Humans to transform the un-harnessed energies into Heavenly abodes.

It is in this context that one must view the evolution of the Emotions. What has been described as Evil is actually the un-harnessed Emotions acting up. Finding methods to overcome rambunctious Emotions has been a major focal point of philosophies and religions through the ages. The evolutionary development of testosterone and estrogen have been a step in this direction that has led us to where we are now—The final step whereby the Emotions accept the discipline of the Standards of Wellness. Do not perceive the "I" as being an unwilling participant. The development of eyesight whereby different entities can view the same thing consistently is but one example of *Her* willingness to cooperate. It is just that *She* was holding out for higher standards.

Many highly academic minds have gathered together for decades sharing thoughts about the Mind of Man. Religious orders around the world meet every ten years to contemplate the plight of Mankind. Physicists join brain researchers. Biologists join Mind researchers. Some physicists are suspicious there is 'something' awry in the Universe, but cannot pinpoint the 'something' or why it is this way.

It is all for the same reason: To try to discover the elusive find that tells Humanity the big picture about how the Mind works or why Life exists. Finding the relationships between the myriad of Man's unanswered questions is a key to understanding the Mind. However, actual knowledge of the Mind's big picture can be revealed as long as there is a willingness to cooperate with *Her*.

Tens of thousands of books are available with pieces of the Mind's big picture. *Lisa Randall, PhD Harvard Physicist once stated that she would like to visit other Life-Forces. Well, we don't visit them; we interact with them twenty-four hours a day, seven days a week. This did not occur serendipitously.* First, we had to realize that an *externally* focused reality could not provide a sanctuary. Second, we had to choose to take an arduous journey *inward* just to survive. And third, we had to flush most of the Universal Conceptualized Truths of an Orderly Newtonian Universe down the toilet. Then, I had to learn the analog language of the Life-Forces through interacting with them. I am still learning this analog language.

Our observations, knowledge, experience, and conclusions are what worked for me and Ronald arising from our Life Learned Lessons. Ronald is a Midwestern tree farmer who had to confront the emotional imbalances of manic-depression and schizophrenia. I am a Navy veteran of the Desert Storm era and an ex-corporate problem solver who also had to confront emotional imbalances involved with a lifelong death-wish. (Now, I feel many of Humanity were also born with a death-wish.)

Yes, our journey was long getting us to Here and Now to solve our mental anguish problems. Along the way, we developed a new emotional immune system. However, as people seek to develop their own uniqueness, the cause behind the Knowledge base about the Mind and Universe will expand exponentially.

When an individual experiences something then that makes it a personal experience. This is how Mankind needs to approach interacting with the Life-Forces that make up their Self. We have personal names for all seven of our Emotions, with Josie being what Ronald affectionately calls his Creativity Emotion who is also the Source of his eloquently written poetry.20 Demonstrating Our Selflessness Shows True Intentions

We were two little girls (3 years apart in age) grappling for our freedom back. Momma lacking self-love was good at pitting us girls against each other. "I'm going to tell momma."

"No, I'm going to tell her!"

Then our fear of her torments and physical abuse forced our silence. Today in the Human-era Awakening-Decade (December 2012-December 2022) my blood-sister and I are separated by the great <u>Head-Divide of Consciousness</u>, I call it. On Martin Luther King Day of 2015 before my daddy's passing, my blood-clotted brain never let me understand what "hospice" meant to prepare me and my soul for this devastation to my heart. To this day, I still have tearful moments during MLK Day. I Know my Daddy is with his Celestial family, being loved beyond measure. I still miss him. I never got to tell him things that I wanted to, but wants of the mind are not always granted without the heart involved.

I think of memories I have lost as being like random-access memory (RAM) of computers, which play "Go Fish" with the brain. Just like a computer, we temporary-home fragments of information into a RAM area of the brain. When given time and Patience, the brain scrambles showing us a bigger picture. Frustrations arise from Ego-expectations unfulfilled, a sign you are moving in the hard direction. Sometimes asking yourself, "Why?" can give you an answer. I now Know the thousands of lessons I had 'chosen' to learn during this incarnation as Christine must have been tremendous. Ones requiring great Courage.

We are all meant to experience Infinite possibilities that we can during this lifetime. Every Observer Being on Earth chose to be here during this time of Humanity's Ascension. It was risky because none of us were going to remember our true identity as soon as we entered human vessel-bodies. It was also risky because we were not going to recall the contract we signed prior to incarnating on Earth. Damn Hard! This planet, out of the Universe entire, offers polarity of experience and duality of Emotions like Earth. For me, according to my numerologist, Ann Perry (YouTube), I also had a massive Karmic debt from previous lives of probably frolic and fun—possibly as a man. Yes, we have all 'tried-on' different sexes, races, religions and body-types and shapes.

Bob Procter once said, "Human's only limitation is Poverty of Imagination." Humans are evolving in our exposing hours. Not all is for naught. Egotism is fading fast, but this will give humans their intelligence. The Laws of Karma ride the waves of the Laws of the Universe. I feel that the Laws of Karma were created for Humanity's balance. Our neurotransmitters require balance and tranquility. It is only the selfish Ego who proclaims our lot is useless. Hogwash! Humanity's Childishness will save the day. Humanity's Childishness tunes us to Source, God-Universe, Peace, Joy, Truth and Unconditional Love.

Aligning with the Childishness of our Subconscious also aligns us to Source, directly to God-Universe. This alignment rids Humanity of Egotism. Evolution asks us to return to our infancy when our innateness was pure, when our innocence felt amazement, awe about everything in life that made us question everything with Joy, Truth, Peace and Unconditional Love. This is the 5th dimension-higher vibration we need to survive the huge shift we are Being asked to make. The 4th dimension-higher vibration is the helpful **dream-state** where the Divine Subconscious can align with you. Learn to Be Responsible for yourself with Duty and Need; let yourself align with childishness and Resolve to align with Truths and Unconditional Love for everything.

Volumes of cosmic radiation pounding Earth as she speeds through space, is freeing Humanity's memories of lower-3rd-dimension vibration from our indebted-karmic lives. This helps us ease into becoming **baby Citizens of the Universe**. Not an easy task. Formidable! That's alright. We can do this together. Let's begin with nothingness, except what's in your **dream-state** imagination. What are you driving, or flying? Where are you going? What are you doing that you always loved to do? Who are you with? What are you wearing? Smelling? Feeling? Sensing?

As we start feeling like Citizens of the Universe, everyday living becomes easier, calm and stress-free as people start functioning with heartfelt purpose. Earth is happily sharing her heart with the **New Humanity**. The contents page of this book should make it easier to see our transition from a list of how energy moves and grows. The 12 Laws of the Universe work together in harmonious rhythms-*turning-into cycles* within our Subconscious as the chariot drivers to God-Universe and life.

So, what does my Subconscious want to tell me today? Three things— *we got your back; the future is being set-up; and run with Freedom when compelled to while out in Nature's beauty* . . . Namaste.

20

NOTHING IS CREATED WITHOUT A PATIENT MINDSET

Our Being is The Observer that which contains our innate Duty and Need energies. Duty has been written about and discussed throughout the laurels of time by the greatest minds of all time. The Great Books of the Western World refer to three different kinds of Duty whereby two of the three have to do with your sense of Duty based on 1—an obligation to someone else or 2—your sense of Duty based upon societal laws. Focus on the third Duty—the one to yourself. Your innate Childishness depends on it. Your Observer Being requires your Duty to always be true to you— period! If not, chaos can begin to build. Your Observer Being also requires your inner innate Needs to be true to you.

The Observer Being can ensure the success of Duty and Need energies by using inner sensors (activated bells and whistles within our bodies) and Observing bodily reactions, such as nervous system reactions of internal or external stimuli. Of course, it behooves the Observing Being at first to Observe **without reacting**. The <u>Great Books Syntopicon I</u> on the subject of Emotion page 326 states, ". . . Though some degree of bodily disturbance would seem to be an essential ingredient in all emotional experience, the intensity and extent of the physiological reverberation, or bodily commotion, is not the same or equal in all the emotions. Some emotions are much more violent than others . . ." Think of a simple life goal/purpose, "to function efficiently with Intent." That is exactly what the Observer Being wants to do—become energy efficient like the very Universe we live in and the planet we live on.

By the year 2200 Earth will be the Garden of Eden once again. As for Humanity, the 2020s and 2030s will likely be chaotic as all changes are. My energy field feels like a tree. Perhaps it is wrapping Humanity? Perhaps it is engulfing everyone's Emotions with unconditional love? Perhaps it is transferring information throughout all of Creation? Perhaps the answer is (e) all of the above for everyone's Subconscious.

Timing is everything. Breakthroughs come with a Patient mindset. Look for Nature's one-two punch when lessons or experiences are repeated twice until Observer Beings understand. Remember Guilt is you are right: Ego is you are Wrong. Humans have always been about 170^0 off-bubble from Nature. It is time to realign ourselves to balance ourselves and heal our bodies from our birth, which will greatly lengthen our lives. It is mind that makes the body rich!

Richard Conn Henry, "Get over it and accept the inarguable conclusion the Universe is immaterial, mental and spiritual." Given the fact everything is energy and <u>we are of our Karmic lives</u>—Cats transmit the same energy as us, making them our mirrors. Dogs transmit the energy that we **receive** from others, making them strainers of energies we pick up from others throughout our day. **Metaphysical Causation** describes the <u>words and thoughts</u> that are creating our experiences.

Never assume you are there just because you are communicating with your Subconscious energies, you interact with them and you finally sleep better than your teenager. All the Emotions have adjustments to make. My Righteous Emotion and Her Humility side, from which self-esteem emerges, had to make the biggest adjustment. The next poem I wrote in 2008.

Counselor's Reckoning

I stepped up to the plate; it was not my Idea.
    Oh God, I am scared—"Why am I here?"
Bombarded by the pitches, I know not where to run,
    but I do not want to die—of what am I afraid?
I was not a heathen in pursuing my quest,
    unknowing that my fate was at the "I"'s behest.

I spent years in anguish and always on the roam,
    trying to kill the distress; there is no place like home.
But home has had some villains, I could not thwart them all.
    Tormented and solemn, I was always at my Christ's call.
Through struggles and lashes I wished not to be afraid
    to step up to the plate, though it was not at my choosing.
But damn it I will survive; it is my heart I'm afraid of losing.
I choose not to run and hide from those bombastic Beings.
I will surpass their judgements: They are not capable of Seeing.
Foolish is their quest to condemn my personal choices,
    as I choose to fly alone to escape from their abuses.
I shall not hate the path I was led on by my Fear;
    I will not sacrifice my heart and those I hold dear.
And when the haunting-memory scoundrels are at last finally dead,
    I shall choose to ignore any *word* thoughts of regret.
For Now I have the feeling of what true Freedom is,
    through Being forced up to the plate—at Creativity's behest.

It was early in 2008 when other dynamic Divinities began appearing in my mind—21 of them to be exact; 21 energies the "I" of the Subconscious allowed me to see. They seem to be the driving forces behind my Emotions. They are also manifestations of the neurotransmitters and chemicals in the body. I used Ronald's religious studies to eventually determine they were referred to as the 24-Elders in the Book of Revelation. We referred to them as the 24 Mothers-of-the-Sisterhood. After the "I" allowed them to show me times in my life they were with me, guiding me. Picking me up when I fell, I became overwhelmed and wrote the following poem.

Mother Purpose

Mother Purpose, elusive you have been.
Lost through the millennia in the Minds of Man.
Battered and tattered you've carried a heavy load,
For your Sister Endeavor to strengthen each abode.
I have been floundering in a life of pain.
Mother Purpose, help me—I cannot do it all again.

Softly whisper to me, wipe away my tears.
Give me a Purpose, cast away my Fears.
We all need a Purpose,
A cause for Man's existence.
Hope and Dread need you,
A cause for Perseverance.

Afterward, the 21 Mothers-of-the-Sisterhood informed me they all wanted to be included in one poem, which Ronald help me write, which my Creativity titled, The Token Male. (Note: originally, we believed there were 21 of these Divine energies, but Wisdom had added a few extra names, in our humble beginnings, until our Beings caught on to the fact several extras were <u>functions of the Beings</u>, Period. Quantum physics has demonstrated that quarks groupings of three entangled energies cannot be separated from the others.

The Token Male

Sometimes, subtleties in the Wind are not so subtle indeed.
The Elders of the Sisterhood are overwhelming Entities to heed.
But each one has a Purpose, an Intent behind their appearance.
Be sensitive within your Heart and Embrace their subtle endurance.

Christ and Lord ATP have aid in their efforts
    to bond Being with the Creativity Emotion.
Appreciation and **Pleasure** are enhanced
    IF earned by way of long-term **Devotion**.

Solace can be found in the **Wisdom**
    of Mother Sophia's vast scope.
Keep Responsibility close to the Heart,
    for **Purpose** of fortifying Dread-Hope.

Through the **Consideration** of others,
Contentment may be found;
Using Doubt instead of Presumption,
Allows **Understanding**'s flow to bound.

Counselor can be an endearingly hard-ass
In Her games of show-and-tell
Righteous and **Humility** both bear this Emotion
When Sara has her doing time in Hell.

Embracing **Fortitude** and **Will**
Can make your Heart grow strong;
For the **Inertia** in Obsession-Sloth
Can put other Emotions where they belong.

Knowledge can be built with **Patience**,
As Ego-Guilt goes about her day;
Be careful with any Judgement,
Lest **Compunction** should correct your way.

Any endeavor will require **Perseverance**,
Bestowing a **Courage** sensation,
For with them Fear is tempered
By your Happiness range of **Elation**.

        Boldfaced names are the Elders of the Sisterhood
        Whose greetings we have learned to Hail,
        But the "I" wanted the Blackness included,
        So they might have a Token Male.

Of course, our Blackness of Awareness is considered the only male energy, because the energy manifested as Lord-ATP arises from the atom's electron-field wavefunction. I was able to see all of them, including my Emotions, for about six months or so until my mind gradually turned black similar to theater lights being turned off a few at a time. Still, Ronald and I interacted with these 21 members of the quantum Sisterhood to uncover more relationships.

Infinity can be used to represent the number of possibilities all of the energies of the Subconscious can combine in relative strengths to make our body and mind. It is vain to concentrate on the makeup of whatever is sensed. Focus on their Intent instead. What is more important is learning to function cohesively with them.

21

WHEREVER YOU GO—THERE YOU ARE!

Aligning with the Childside of our Subconscious also aligns us to Source, directly to God-Universe. This alignment rids Humanity of Egotism. Evolution asks us to return to our infancy when our innateness was pure, when our innocence felt amazement, awe about everything in life that made us question everything with Joy, Truth, Peace and Unconditional Love. This is the 5th dimension-higher (a broad range of wavelengths) vibrations that we need to survive a huge shift we are asked to make. The 4th dimension-higher vibration is the helpful **dream-state** where the Divine Subconscious can align with you. Learn to Be Responsible for yourself with Duty and Need; let yourself align with childishness and Resolve to align with Truths and Unconditional Love for everything.

Volumes of cosmic radiation pounding Earth as she speeds through space, is freeing Humanity's memories of lower-3rd-dimension vibration from our indebted-karmic lives. This helps us ease into becoming **baby Citizens of the Universe**. Not an easy task. Formidable! That's alright. We can do this together. Let's begin with nothingness, except what's in your **dream-state** imagination. What are you driving, or flying? Where are you going? What are you doing that you always loved to do? Who are you with? What are you wearing? Smelling? Feeling? Sensing?

As we start feeling like Citizens of the Universe, everyday living becomes easier, calm and stress-free as people start functioning with heartfelt purpose. Earth is happily sharing her heart with the **New Humanity**. The contents page of this book should make it easier to see our transition from a list of how energy moves and grows. The 12 Laws of the Universe work together in harmonious rhythms-*turning-into cycles* within our Subconscious as the chariot drivers to God-Universe and life.

The subject of Mind in the Encyclopedia Britannica's Great Books Syntopicon II, page 141 states, "*. . . thinking goes beyond sensing, either as an elaboration of the materials of sense or as an apprehension of objects which are totally beyond the reach of sense.*"

Saint Thomas Aquinas (1225-1274) states, "For the intellect to understand actually . . . there is a need for the act of the imagination and of the other powers . . . that are acts of bodily organs."

Mind has three functions:

1. thinking or thought, although I find the quiet to be Peaceful right now, knowing that nothing lasts forever;
2. Knowledge that is growth for the brain or Knowing that is growth for our vessel receptors and senses we can tune into and;
3. purpose or Intention; "*it is rather on the level of the behavior of the living things that purpose seems to require a factor over and above the sense, limited as they are to present appearances. It cannot be found in the passions which have the same limitation as the sense, for unless they are checked they tend toward immediate emotional discharge.*" (Great Books Syntopicon II, page 141)

While the Great Books cover the subject of Mind in over 300-400 references including the writings of Plato and Aristotle up to and including the writings of Freud, the Subconscious as containing seven Emotions has not been addressed until now—oddly at the end of Earth's 26,000 year cycle. Many psychologists have written books about our Childside, i.e. Our Inner Child by Dr. Joyce Mills. Our Childside's inquisitiveness inside us all is the Subconscious mind's ability to function efficiently—IF allowed to come out and play.

22

EVERYTHING IS SOMEHOW CONNECTED

"There are only seven Emotions, but because of their dualities, relative strengths and multitasking, they will put the 'temporary home' technique to the test. One can only sense one Emotion at a time—the exception is the Righteous-Humility Emotion who you can sense both Her Righteous side and Her Humility side. The seven Emotions are responsible for most of how we Feel. Because of the wide range in their strength, the number of combinations approach infinity. All seven also combine for anxiety, with stress being just another octave of the seven. I personally know of five levels, but they normally only function in three. Emotional intoxication is difficult to describe. I'm like a Supreme Court Justice commenting on pornography, 'I know it when I see it'. There is also the matter of the caustic Emotions functioning as the strange attractors of goodness, ignorance and passion which are described in detail in the Bhagavad-Gita: The Goodness and Superstitions of Religions the resulting ignorance of prejudices, and need I expound about Egotism and Vanity? Everyone is under their influence. Even with my Knowing loving my Emotions, I still must deal with their sporadic pull in their role as strange attractors. However, there is a new attractor arising that leads to Emotional Sobriety and functions as a new source of motivation for Humanity—the 4-Children of Innocence (our Being's—Duty & Need; our Creativity's—Childside and Resolve)" Written by my friend, Ronald Grafton

FEAR inside our minds and bodies shut off our immune system. Yes—OFF completely. Fear puts our bodies in a state of flight and/or fight, and since the body cannot heal us at the same time, shuts down our immune system just like stress or fretting over depression. Beings CHOOSE whether to feel the stressor or not. But when it comes to flight or fight, the adrenaline rush is taken under the control of our Subconscious that shuts OFF consciousness and takes over the self-preservation. Given that our hearts are 5,000 times more powerful than our minds, the Subconscious is our direct link to our hearts and God-Universe (Source).

LIES/DECEITS are everywhere but our build-in lie-detectors are also OFF. Humans are pre-programmed to take in all stimuli around us without prejudice and allowing time to pass before placing importance on things we experience or information we have heard. This is called information incubation, which is required for all new Knowledge. Everything energy in the Universe has an incubation timeframe before setting seed or manifesting.

HATE is an Emotion of our Childishness that can be felt by young and old alike to protect our quantum self from harm. This Childishness is the inner faith that we can do anything! Childishness is best described by a song of music group, (YouTube) FEARLESS SOUL, called "Thoughts Become Things" and because its words ring TRUTH, I would like to share some with you—(It is probably best to hear the song for yourself on YouTube, search— FEARLESS SOUL music for song titled— <u>THOUGHTS BECOME THINGS.</u>

Observer Beings—literally everything in the Universe is wavelengths / energy. Everything about Humanity is energy—good or bad. As a whole I prefer to think of Humanity as good but possibilities are not so cut and dry as that, because Egotism still exists.

> *"For I say, through the Grace given unto me, to every man that is among you, to think of himself more highly than he ought to think; but to think soberly**, according as God hath dealt to every man the measure of faith*."* (Romans 12:1-3)
>
> *FAITH IN SELF; **SOBERLY to our Subconscious Emotions is meant as—**Balance.**

Every one of our Emotions has experienced the same as you, Observer Beings. Hence, your Emotions give you plenty of head noise that Science predicts some 70,000-80,000 thoughts per day.

- Balanced Emotions takes focus, Beautiful Souls.
- Balanced Emotions bring Peace, Joy, Truth and Unconditional Love with direct link to Source.
- To get through the inner focus needed to find Balance, you might cry and not yet know why?
- OBSERVE—You may have words spill from your lips not knowing where they come from?
- OBSERVE—You might have many experiences you cannot explain **while** you are experiencing them?
- Keep ASKING questions, and keep asking until the answers start making your heart flutter?

Observer Beings because with FAITH in yourself, you can find the answers you are seeking. Also, keep the twelve Laws of the Universe in mind and heart to receive consistent ABUNDANCE that is available to each of Humanity.

23

THE BEST REWARD IS CONTRIBUTING TO THE WHOLE

Devotional Service, poem by *little chrissy*

Christ invited the Sisterhood of Elders to come into our Heart; an overwhelming plethora of feelings, as my Emotions played their part. When my Happiness stayed with Creativity, Happy tears is what I promptly felt, like Niagara's Waters flowing and my Heart began to melt.

The lightness of my Heart made Hope's essence strong. The coming of a future event is not where Fear will belong, *"As the even begins to unfold, do not be overwhelmed,"* Christ said, *"You will need clarity of thought, relieve your tired head."*

"It is a gift from the Elders for all your hard work. That you may continue with Endeavors, your Duty you must not shirk. For you are employed by the Elders—within you they now reside. Flow with their overwhelming presence, allow they to be your guide."

The ultimate Devotional Service to 21 of the Divinities from the Atom: Their Intent behind my writings is more than I can fathom. After decades of Being manic, my pen I will not still, to say what is deep in my Heart, *"This ain't no damn drill."*

The Waters of the Sisterhood will flow upon the Earth to save the decaying
atom for whatever Life is worth. So, when any ghostly apparitions
appear and say hello to you, Embrace the ultimate Devotional Service,
then perhaps Hope and Purpose will find you, too.

The possibility of Divinities being involved, manifested through our
main seven neurotransmitters inside us is something I Know through
experience with them. So Be it is the same for my dear friend and Celestial
brother, Ronald Grafton. This book came about from hundreds of files
on my computer that have been written and saved since 2006 about the
Subconscious, although many of them I don't remember writing, probably
because of my 2015 stroke.

Nonetheless, I am who I have learned I am from data collected off
of YouTube videos, including Ann Perry's numerology report. (Thank
You, Ann) I am a Heyoka Empath who respects free will, grasps duality
of Humanity and challenges Egotism by mirroring it back to people.
Through living many challenging experiences, I can humbly say that
walking in someone else's shoes became easy. I call it WHAT IT IS. I feel
psychologically strong, emotionally resilient because I am at Peace with my
Emotions. Thanks to my friend, Ronald Grafton's poetry. Additionally, I
tip my hat to Anita Moorjani who had no one to turn to for support with
her Subconscious after her near-death experience. God Bless you, Anita!

My Duty to Humanity is to assist your Awakening, Beautiful Beings.
The world will come to you, America, to heal your young hearts, to spread
unconditional love for your struggles of Being a young country. You can
share your own Joy after you remember what Joy feels like, and recognize
Joy for the Elation that you feel. Joy is home vibrating beacons of love to
Celestial families. Joy is vibrating home beacons of unconditional love to
God-Consciousness, to Universal Mind.

My journey has been arduous beyond imagination, Lifepath 5, and yet
I had signed up for it all while putting many challenging lessons behind
me. Today, I have unconditional love for myself, every person, plant and
pets of the animal kingdom. It feels peaceful 99% of the time while Earth
speeds through space, a blessing of Life. I have no Fear for my Emotion of
Fear will warn me of real danger. If I am to catch COVID19, then I can See
it staying for no longer than 19 seconds. It cannot survive in the higher-
dimensional vibration of unconditional Love.

Childishness to our vessel-body system is like golden honey, the unconditional-love adamant particles of God-Universe healing. Adamant particles are Nature's infinite wavelengths—our infinite pharmaceuticals inside us. This is the reason fake pharmaceutical prescriptions will vanish completely within 30-40 years.

Namaste, 'little chrissy' with Peace, Joy, Truth and Unconditional Love for Humanity . . .

Wisdom Addendum For Periods of Gloom

I have included these lessons from General Colin Powell that I thankfully obtained after Dessert Storm (the 1990s), because they helped me in times of darkness with the Subconscious more than I can express. Perhaps these lessons can help you too, Dear Observer Being. Read them often, when needed, especially if you need to be RE-CENTERED IN YOUR HEART!

"Leadership is the art of accomplishing more than the science of management says is possible."
Leadership Lessons from General Colin Powell

Lesson 1: *"Being responsible sometimes means pissing people off."* Good leadership involves responsibility to the welfare of the group, which means that some people will get angry at your actions and decisions. It's inevitable, if you're honorable. Trying to get everyone to like you is a sign of mediocrity: you'll avoid the tough decisions, you'll avoid confronting the people who need to be confronted, and you'll avoid offering differential rewards based on differential performance because some people might get upset. Ironically, by procrastinating on the difficult choices, by trying not to get anyone mad, and by treating everyone equally 'nicely' regardless of their contributions, you'll simply ensure that the only people you'll wind up angering are the most creative and productive people in the organization.

Lesson 2: *"The day soldiers stop bringing you their problems is the day you have stopped leading them. They have either lost confidence that you can help*

them or concluded that you do not care. Either case is a failure of leadership."
If this were a litmus test, the majority of CEOs would fail. One, they build
so many barriers to upward communication that the very idea of someone
lower in the hierarchy looking up to the leader for help is ludicrous. Two,
the corporate culture they foster often defines asking for help as weakness
or failure, so people cover up their gaps, and the organization suffers
accordingly. Real leaders make themselves accessible and available. They
show concern for the efforts and challenges faced by underlings, even as
they demand high standards. Accordingly, they are more likely to create
an environment where problem analysis replaces blame.

Lesson 3: *"Don't be buffaloed by experts and elites. Experts often possess
more data than judgment. Elites can become so inbred that they produce
hemophiliacs who bleed to death as soon as they are nicked by the real world."*
Small companies and start-ups don't have the time for analytically detached
experts. They don't have the money to subsidize lofty elites, either. The
president answers the phone and drives the truck when necessary; everyone
on the payroll visibly produces and contributes to bottom-line results or
they're history. But as companies get bigger, they often forget who 'brought
them to the dance': things like all-hands involvement, egalitarianism,
informality, market intimacy, daring, risk, speed, agility. Policies that
emanate from ivory towers often have an adverse impact on the people out
in the field who are fighting the wars or bringing in the revenues. Real
leaders are vigilant, and combative, in the face of these trends.

Lesson 4: *"Do"t be afraid to challenge the pros, even in their own
backyard."* Learn from the pros, observe them, seek them out as mentors
and partners. But remember that even the pros may have leveled out in
terms of their learning and skills. Sometimes even the pros can become
complacent and lazy. Leadership does not emerge from blind obedience to
anyone. Xerox's Barry Rand was right on target when he warned his people
that if you have a yes-man working for you, one of you is redundant. Good
leadership encourages everyone's evolution.

Lesson 5: *"Never neglect details. When everyone's mind is dulled or
distracted the leader must be doubly vigilant."* Strategy equals execution.
All the great ideas and visions in the world are worthless if they can't be
implemented rapidly and efficiently. Good leaders delegate and empower
others liberally, but they pay attention to details, every day. (Think about

supreme athletic coaches like Jimmy Johnson, Pat Riley and Tony La Russa). Bad ones, even those who fancy themselves as progressive "visionaries," think they're somehow "above" operational details. Paradoxically, good leaders understand something else: an obsessive routine in carrying out the details begets conformity and complacency, which in turn dulls everyone's mind. That is why even as they pay attention to details, they continually encourage people to challenge the process. They implicitly understand the sentiment of CEO leaders like Quad Graphic's Harry Quadracchi, Oticon's Lars Kolind and the late Bill McGowan of MCI, who all independently asserted that the Job of a leader is not to be the chief organizer, but the chief disorganizer.

Lesson 6: *"You don't know what you can get away with until you try."* You know the expression, "it's easier to get forgiveness than permission." Well, it's true. Good leaders don't wait for official blessing to try things out. They're prudent, not reckless. But they also realize a fact of life in most organizations: if you ask enough people for permission, you'll inevitably come up against someone who believes his job is to say "no." So the moral is, don't ask. Less effective middle managers endorsed the sentiment, "If I haven't explicitly been told "YES, I CAN'T DO IT," whereas the good ones believed, "If I haven't explicitly been told NO, I can." There's a world of difference between these two points of view.

Lesson 7 *"Keep looking below surface appearances. Don't shrink from doing so (just) because you might not like what you find."* "If it ain't broke, don't fix it" is the slogan of the complacent, the arrogant or the scared. It's an excuse for inaction, a call to non-arms. It's a mind-set that assumes (or hopes) that today's realities will continue tomorrow in a tidy, linear and predictable fashion. Pure fantasy. In this sort of culture, you won't find people who pro-actively take steps to solve problems as they emerge. Here's a little tip: don't invest in these companies.

Lesson 8 *"Organization doesn't really accomplish anything. Plans don't accomplish anything, either. Theories of management don't much matter. Endeavors succeed or fail because of the people involved. Only by attracting the best people will you accomplish great deeds."* In a brain-based economy, your best assets are people. We've heard this expression so often that it's become trite. But how many leaders really "walk the talk" with this stuff? Too often, people are assumed to be empty chess pieces to be moved around by grand viziers, which may explain why so many top managers immerse their calendar time in deal making, restructuring and the latest management fad. How many immerse themselves in the goal of creating an environment where the best, the brightest, the most creative are attracted, retained and, most importantly, unleashed?

Lesson 9 *"Organization charts and fancy titles count for next to nothing."* Organization charts are frozen, anachronistic photos in a work place that ought to be as dynamic as the external environment around you. If people really followed organization charts, companies would collapse. In well-run organizations, titles are also pretty meaningless. At best, they advertise some authority, an official status conferring the ability to give orders and induce obedience. But titles mean little in terms of real power, which is the capacity to influence and inspire. Have you ever noticed that people will personally commit to certain individuals who on paper (or on the organization chart) possess little authority, but instead possess pizzazz, drive, expertise, and genuine caring for teammates and products? On the flip side, non-leaders in management may be formally anointed with all the perks and frills associated with high positions, but they have little influence on others, apart from their ability to extract minimal compliance to minimal standards.

Lesson 10 *"Never let your ego get so close to your position that when your position goes, your ego goes with it."* Too often, change is stifled by people who cling to familiar turfs and job descriptions. One reason that even large organizations wither is that managers won't challenge old, comfortable ways of doing things. But real leaders understand that, nowadays, every one of our jobs is becoming obsolete. The proper response is to obsolete our activities before someone else does. Effective leaders create a climate where people's worth is determined by their willingness to learn new skills and grab new responsibilities, thus perpetually reinventing their jobs. The most important question in performance evaluation becomes not, "How well did you perform your job since the last time we met?" but, "How much did you change it?"

Lesson 11 *"Fit no stereotypes. Don't chase the latest management fads. The situation dictates which approach best accomplishes the team's mission."* Flitting from fad to fad creates team confusion, reduces the leader's credibility, and drains organizational coffers. Blindly following a particular fad generates rigidity in thought and action. Sometimes speed to market is more important than total quality. Sometimes an unapologetic directive is more appropriate than participatory discussion. Some situations require the leader to hover closely; others require long, loose leashes. Leaders honor their core values, but they are flexible in how they execute them. They understand that management techniques are not magic mantras but simply tools to be reached for at the right times.

Lesson 12 *"Perpetual optimism is a force multiplier."* The ripple effect of a leader's enthusiasm and optimism is awesome. So is the impact of cynicism and pessimism. Leaders who whine and blame engender those same behaviors among their colleagues. I am not talking about stoically accepting organizational stupidity and performance incompetence with a "what, me worry?" smile. I am talking about a gung-ho attitude that says "we can change things here, we can achieve awesome goals, we can be the best." Spare me the grim litany of the "realist," give me the unrealistic aspirations of the optimist any day.

Lesson 13 *"Powell's Rules for Picking People:"* Look for intelligence and judgment, and most critically, a capacity to anticipate, to see around corners. Also look for loyalty, integrity, a high energy drive, a balanced ego, and the drive to get things done. How often do our recruitment and hiring processes tap into these attributes? More often than not, we ignore them in favor of length of resume, degrees and prior titles. A string of job descriptions a recruit held yesterday seem to be more important than who one is today, what they can contribute tomorrow, or how well their values mesh with those of the organization. You can train a bright, willing novice in the fundamentals of your business fairly readily, but it's a lot harder to train someone to have integrity, judgment, energy, balance, and the drive to get things done. Good leaders stack the deck in their favor right in the recruitment phase.

Lesson 14 *"Great leaders are almost always great simplifiers, who can cut through argument, debate and doubt, to offer a solution everybody can understand."* Effective leaders understand the KISS principle, Keep It Simple, Stupid. They articulate vivid, over-arching goals and values, which they use to drive daily behaviors and choices among competing alternatives. Their visions and priorities are lean and compelling, not cluttered and buzzword-laden. Their decisions are crisp and clear, not tentative and ambiguous. They convey an unwavering firmness and consistency in their actions, aligned with the picture of the future they paint. The result: clarity of purpose, credibility of leadership, and integrity in organization.

Lesson 15 *Part I: "Use the formula P=40 to 70, in which P stands for the probability of success and the numbers indicate the percentage of information acquired."*

Part II: "Once the information is in the 40 to 70 range, go with your gut." Don't take action if you have only enough information to give you less than a 40 percent chance of being right, but don't wait until you have enough facts to be 100 percent sure, because by then it is almost always too late. Today, excessive delays in the name of information-gathering breeds "analysis paralysis." Procrastination in the name of reducing risk actually increases risk.

Lesson 16 *"The commander in the field is always right and the rear echelon is wrong, unless proved otherwise."* Too often, the reverse defines corporate culture. This is one of the main reasons why leaders like Ken Iverson of Nucor Steel, Percy Barnevik of Asea Brown Boveri, and Richard Branson of Virgin have kept their corporate staffs to a bare-bones minimum - how about fewer than 100 central corporate staffers for global $30 billion-plus ABB? Or around 25 and 3 for multi-billion Nucor and Virgin, respectively? Shift the power and the financial accountability to the folks who are bringing in the beans, not the ones who are counting or analyzing them.

Lesson 17 "Have fun in your command. Don't always run at a breakneck pace. Take leave when you've earned it: Spend time with your families. Corollary: surround yourself with people who take their work seriously, but not themselves, those who work hard and play hard." Herb Kelleher of Southwest Air and Anita Roddick of The Body Shop would agree: seek people who have some balance in their lives, who are fun to hang out with, who like to laugh (at themselves, too) and who have some non-job priorities which they approach with the same passion that they do their work. Spare me the grim workaholic or the pompous pretentious "professional;" I'll help them find jobs with my competitor.

Lesson 18 *"Command is lonely."* Harry Truman was right. Whether you're a CEO or the temporary head of a project team, the buck stops here. You can encourage participative management and bottom-up employee involvement, but ultimately the essence of leadership is the willingness to make the tough, unambiguous choices that will have an impact on the fate of the organization. I've seen too many non-leaders flinch from this responsibility. Even as you create an informal, open, collaborative corporate culture, prepare to be lonely.

"I" am Addendum

I consider any document to be of great importance if extreme measure was taken to preserve the text for millennia, regardless of whether it was written in a chaotic form. First drafts of any writing usually are chaotic and ancient documents appear no different. Our ancestors had to write everything out by hand, which made correcting first drafts of anything tedious and time consuming.

The Thunder: Perfect Mind is my favorite ancient document because it was the most difficult to decipher. Although it is over 1,700 years old, it expresses our current tumultuous times of near-insanity shootings and missed perceptions of reality.

I will present the text a piece at a time and in a chaotic order from its original form. Regardless of how I viewed the text to see it in a brand new way didn't matter, because my *fill-in-the-blanks where the papyrus was too decayed* were channeled from Source. And regardless of how elusive the document's meaning had been since its discovery in 1945 as part of the Nag Hammadi Library in English, I tip my hat to its ancient scribe for the pure beauty of it, who had probably also channeled this text from Source!

The Thunder: Perfect Mind (deciphered)
Where "I" AM came from

"I" was sent forth from the power. [the *power* is $E=MC^2$]
"I" AM of the creation of the spirits.
"I" AM appearance at the request of the souls [**Beings**].
"I" AM the sign of the letter and the designation of the division, and "I" reflect on the designation, and the light is the division.

And my power is from him, and he is my offspring in due time.
And the power of the powers in my knowledge of the angels [**Emotions**]
    who have been sent at my word,
    and of gods in their seasons by my counsel,
    and of spirits of every man who exists with me,
    and of women who dwell within me.
"I" AM the staff of his power in his youth,
    and he is the rod of my old age,
    and whatever he wills happens to me. [**insinuates a phase shift
    in these last 3 lines**]

INFINITE **opposites of power pre-wired in our brains**

And those who have not known me let them know me.
"I" AM unlearned, and they learn from me.
For "I" AM knowledge and ignorance
"I" AM the one who is disgraced and the great one.
"I" AM control and the uncontrollable.
"I" AM the union and the dissolution.
"I" AM the abiding and "I" AM the dissolving.
"I" AM the honored one and the scorned one.
"I" AM she whose wedding is great and "I" have not taken a husband.
"I" AM the whore and the holy one.
"I" AM the wife and the virgin.
"I" AM the mother and the daughter.
"I" AM the members of my mother.
"I" AM the barren one and many are her sons.
"I" AM the midwife and she who does not bear.
"I" AM the solace of my labor pains.
"I" AM the bride and the bridegroom.
"I" AM the mother of my father and the sister of my husband.
"I" AM she who is weak and "I" AM well in a pleasant place.
"I" AM senseless and "I" AM wise.
"I" AM the one whom you have scattered, [**as in <u>scattering ideas</u>**]
    and you have gathered me together. [**as in *collecting ideas***]
"I" AM shame and boldness: "I" AM shameless: "I" AM ashamed.

"I" AM strength and "I" AM Fear: "I" AM war and peace.
"I" AM the one before whom you have been ashamed,
    and you have been shameless to me.
And "I" have come to those who reflect upon me.
And "I" have been found among those who seek after me.

Her Attributes no matter what you believe

"I" AM the hearing which is attainable to everyone
    and the speech which cannot be grasped.
"I" AM a mute who does not speak,
    and great is my multitude of words.
For "I" AM the one who alone exists,
    and "I" have no one who will judge me.
"I" AM the utterance of my name.
"I" AM the silence that is incomprehensible
    and the idea whose remembrance is frequent.
"I" AM the voice whose sound is manifold
    and the word whose appearance is multiple.
"I" AM the one who has been hated everywhere
    and who has been loved everywhere.
"I" AM the name of the sound and the sound of the name.
"I" AM she who does not keep festival,
    and "I" AM she whose festivals are many.
"I", "I" AM godless, and "I" AM the one whose God is great.
"I" AM the judgment of the Greeks and of the barbarians.
"I" AM the one whose image is great in Egypt
    and the one who has no image among the barbarians.
"I" AM she who cries out,
    and "I" AM cast forth upon the face of the earth.
"I" AM the one who cries out and "I" listen.
"I" prepare the bread and my Mind within.
"I" AM the knowledge of my name.

Her Message to the Secret Societies

"I" AM the knowledge of my inquiry,
    and the finding of those who seek after me,
    and the command of those who ask of me.
Those who are close to me have been ignorant of me,
    and those who are far away from me
    are the ones who have known me.
You who know me, be ignorant of me.
Do not be arrogant to me when "I" AM cast out upon the earth,
    and you will find me in those that are to come.
And do not look upon me when "I" AM cast out
    among those who are disgraced
    and in the least places, nor laugh at me.
And do not look upon me on the dung-heap
    nor go and leave me cast out.
And you will find me in the kingdoms.
For "I" AM the wisdom of the Greeks
    and the knowledge of the barbarians.
"I" AM the one whom they call Life, and you have called Death.
On the day when "I" AM close to you, you are far away from me.
And on the day when "I" AM far away from you "I" AM close to you.
But whenever you hide yourselves, "I" myself will appear,
For whenever you appear, "I" myself will hide from you.
Those who have <u>appeared</u> to it* <u>hide</u> senselessly <u>from it</u>.
Why have you hated me in your counsels
    for "I" shall be silent among those who are silent
    and "I" shall appear and speak?
(*the "it" is <u>Actuality</u>)

Man's Ego Response of "I" Through the Ages

You who are vanquished*, judge them who vanquished you
    before they give judgment against you,
    because the judge and partiality exist in you:

If you are condemned by this one,
  who will acquit you?
Or if you are acquitted by this one,
  who will be able to detain you?
Why do you curse me and honor me,
  for you have wounded and you have had mercy?
You honor me you hearers and you whisper against me;
"I" AM iniquity within; "I" am Truth of the natures.
"I" AM she whose festivals are many,
  and "I" AM she who does not keep festival.
"I" AM the one whose God is great and "I", "I" am godless.
"I" AM the one whom you have hidden from, and you appear to me.
For why do you despise my fear and curse my pride,
  for "I" AM she who exists in all Fears and strength in trembling?
"I" AM the one whom you have despised, and you reflect upon me.
"I" AM the one whom you have reflected upon,
  and you have scorned me.
Why then have you hated me, you Greeks
  because "I" AM a barbarian among the barbarians?

(*forced from the Subconscious)
Her Perspective of Humanity

Those who are without association with me are ignorant of me.
Why, you who hate me, do you love me, and hate those who love me?
You who deny me, confess me, and you who confess me, deny me.
You who tell the truth about me, lie about me.
And you who have lied about me, tell the truth about me.
And what you see outside of you, you see inside of you.
It is visible and it is your garment because:
  "I" AM the Mind of everyone and the rest of no one.
For many are the pleasant forms which exist in **numerous sins [from Egotism]**,
  and **incontinencies**,
  and **disgraceful passions**,
  and **fleeting pleasures**,

171

Which men embrace until they become sober [BALANCED]
    and go up ['up' is a decoy, should be down to low-energy state]
        to their **resting place**.
[Resting place is meant as Heaven on Earth in the Garden of Eden within the Subconscious mind.

Adjusting Humanity's Perspective of the "I" AM

Give heed to me.
Judge them before they give judgment against you.
If you are condemned by this one, who will acquit you
    because the judge and partiality exist in you
Do not be ignorant of me.
"I" AM the one below, and they come up to me.
You honor me and you whisper against me.
Look then at his words and all the writings
    which have been completed.
For what is inside of you is what is outside of you,
    and the one who fashions you on the outside
        is the one who shaped the inside of you.

Preparing for the Veil to Lift

Be on your guard!
Hear me, you hearers, and learn of my words, you who know me.
Do not be ignorant of me anywhere or any time.
And do not make your voice hate me, nor your hearing.
And do not cast me out among those who are slain in violence,
For "I", "I" AM compassionate and "I" AM cruel.
And do not cast anyone out nor turn anyone away
    should <u>they</u> turn you away and <u>they</u> know him not.
<u>Know him.</u> [The Blackness of Awareness]
What is mine <u>is his and his is mine</u>.
"I" AM the judgment and the acquittal.
"I", "I" AM sinless, and the root of sin **[Egotism]** derives from me.

"I" AM lust [**Egotism**]in outward appearance,

and interior self-control exists within me.

Be on your guard!

Hear me in gentleness, and learn of me in roughness [**tough love**].

"I" AM the one who provides the defense and the criticism.

"I" AM the one who is called Truth and iniquity is found.

Give heed then, you hearers and you also,

the angels and those who have been sent,

and you spirits who have arisen from the dead.

Be on your guard!

Do not hate my obedience and do not love my self-control.

In my weakness, do not forsake me, and do not be afraid of my power.

Come forward to childhood.

And do not despise it because it is small and it is little.

And do not turn away greatnesses in some part from the smallnesses.

For the smallnesses are known from the greatnesses.

After the Veil Lifts . . .

Listen hearers and "I" will come to you from the great power,

and the sound will not move the name.

"I" appear and will walk in with the seal of my offspring.

And those who are in my substance are the ones who know me.

Do not separate me from the first ones whom you have known,

And listen to the one who created me,

and "I" will speak his name.

You who are waiting for me, take me to yourselves,

and do not banish me from your sight.

Take me to yourselves with understanding from grief,

and take me to yourselves from understanding with grief.

And take me to yourselves from places that are ugly and in ruin,

and rob from those which are good even though in ugliness:

Out of shame, take me to yourselves shamelessly;

and out of shamelessness and shame,

upbraid my members in yourselves.

Look upon me, you who reflect upon me,
 and you hearers, hear me.
And come forward to me, you who know me
 and you who know my members,
  and establish the great ones <u>among the small first creatures</u> [our
  INNATE Duty, Need, Childishness & Resolve].
And they will find me there, and they will live,
 and they will not die again.

Acknowledgements

I would like to thank the editors and publisher of _The Nag Hammadi Library in English_, 3rd edition. I am humbly grateful for all the hard work and long hours put forth to make the ancient texts available to everyone since their unearthing in 1945. I also wish to thank writers of all genres and individuals who provided fractals of information throughout my life of research allowing this book to be written. If I have left anyone off of this list, then I am humbly sorry.

Ronald W. Grafton, Poet and dear friend of mine. Thank you, Ron and God Bless YOU!

United States Navy for their exemplary electronics training that allowed me to understand intricacies of quantum physics.

General Colin Powell, commander of Desert Storm during my Navy enlistment, whose _18 Lessons on Leadership_ are just as applicable for functioning within the subconscious mind as they are in everyday life.

United States Army for an internet copy of their training series book, _Bastogne: The Story of the First Eight Days in which the 101st Airborne Division Was Closed Within the Ring of German Forces_, by Colonel S.L.A. Marshall, 1946.

Ben Stein for his documentary _Expelled! No Intelligence Allowed_, which identifies the disaffected people

Stephen Hawking and Leonard Mlodinow for their 'marvelously concise book on physics *The Grand Design.*

Stephen MacKenna and B.S. Page for their translation and internet copy of Plotinus' Enneads for which I appreciate more than I can begin to express.

Mark Booth, whose book, *The Secret History of the World as Laid Down by the Secret Societies*, allowed me to see aspects of my own life in a broader historical perspective.

Carlos Castaneda for his books about Yaqui shaman don Juan Matus.

John Horgan for his book *Rational Mysticism, and whose subconscious mind surfaced, if only for a brief moment in time, in 1981*

Julian Jaynes' *The Origin of Consciousness in the Breakdown of the Bicameral Mind*

Steven Pinker for his general writings and acknowledging the *executive "I"* of our Mind makes the final decision.

R. Douglas Fields and **Colleagues** for their research showing ATP and adenosine are main messengers in our brain, and for R. Douglas Fields' book *The Other Brain*

Dr. Henry Han, Dr. Glenn E. Miller and Nancy Deville for their informative and well-written book *Ancient Herbs, Modern Medicine*

Michael Shermer for his Skepticism expressed in his articles in *Scientific American* magazine

Zachary Shore for his book *Blunder-Why Smart People Make Bad Decisions*

Dr. Karen Nesbitt Shanor for her book *The Emerging Mind*

Dr. Deepak Chopra for his insightful chapter in *The Emerging Mind*

Dr. Joe Dispenza for his books *Breaking the Habit of Being Yourself and Becoming Supernatural*

Dr. David R. Hawkins for his book *Power VS. Force—The Hidden Determinants of Human Behavior*

Dr. Norma J. Milanovich for her book *We, The Arcturians*

Dr. Richard Gerber for his book *Vibrational Medicine—The #1 Handbook of Subtle-Energy Therapies*

Dr. Alberto Villoldo for his book *Grow a New Body—How SPIRIT and Power Plant NUTRIENTS Can Transform Your Health*

Jean Carper for her book *Your Miracle Brain*

Dr. Henry Han, Dr. Glenn E. Miller, and Nancy Deville for their in-depth book *Ancient Herbs, Modern Medicine: Improving Your Health by combining Chinese Herbal Medicine and Western Medicine*

The memory of Ron L. Hubbard for his lifetime of research and development of Dianetics and Scientology, as well as the millions of Scientologists world-wide who can help prepare people for the *Apocalypse*. Deep regrets and apologies to narcissists who hijacked his lifetime of work.

Dr. E. Fuller Torrey for his book *Surviving Schizophrenia*, which expresses excellent observations on the effects of schizophrenia.

A.C. Bhaktivedanta—*Bhagavad-Gita As It Is*

Hal Lindsey—critical analysis of *Revelation* 2 & 3

James Gleick—*Chaos, Making a New Science*

Jim Al-Khalili—*Quantum, A Guide for the Perplexed*

Sir Roger Penrose—lowest energy states

Tim Folger and Susan Kruglinski—photon superposition

Lisa Randall, Harvard Physicist—closed-string graviton

Richard P. Feynman—quantum electrodynamics/QED

NOTE: All _Book of Revelation_ quotes are from a 1971 Reader's Digest King James Version

Printed in the United States
By Bookmasters